LIVING WITH YOUR TEENAGE DAUGHTER AND LIKING IT!

A SITUATION-BY-SITUATION GUIDE TO ENJOYING YOUR DAUGHTER'S ADOLESCENCE

Meryl Fishman and Kathleen Horwich

A FIRESIDE BOOK
Published by Simon and Schuster
New York

Copyright © 1983 by Meryl Fishman and Kathleen Horwich
All rights reserved
including the right of reproduction
in whole or in part in any form
A Fireside Book
Published by Simon and Schuster
A Division of Gulf & Western Corporation
Simon & Schuster Building
Rockefeller Center
1230 Avenue of the Americas
New York, New York 10020
FIRESIDE and colophon are registered trademarks of Simon & Schuster
Designed by Elaine Golt Gongora
Manufactured in the United States of America
10 9 8 7 6 5 4 3 2 1
Library of Congress Cataloging in Publication Data
Fishman, Meryl,
    Living with your teenage daughter and liking it.

    "A Fireside book."
    Includes index.
    1. Daughters.   2. Adolescent girls.   3. Mothers and daughters.
4. Parenting.   I. Horwich, Kathleen,   II. Title.
HQ777.F55 1983   649′.125   82–19564
ISBN: 0-671-46880-4

CONTENTS

CONTENTS

To our daughters

AUTHORS' NOTE

This book is written as if by one author, but in fact it is the compilation of the thoughts, feelings and experiences of two women and their many friends and acquaintances who are or have been the parents of adolescent daughters. You may agree or disagree with some or all of the positions expressed; you may even find some ideas offensive. However, it is not the intent of the authors to advocate a particular moral or ethical viewpoint. The authors' beliefs are expressed only as an example of how to integrate individual views and values into the overall resolution of parent-child conflicts.

FOREWORD

I like this book. It contains many of the things I have been saying about teenagers for the past ten years in my own books. Not surprisingly, I think those sections are splendid. It also contains other sections that are contrary to what I believe about the behavior of teenagers and how it can best be coped with. Naturally, I think those sections are incorrect. You probably will not agree with all of this. As I mentioned, I don't either. But you will learn a great deal from it. This book, written by two non-psychologists, mothers of teenagers, is far more refreshing and illuminating than most of the books I have read in the past ten years written by psychologists about teenage behavior. These mothers have been there. They know the territory.

This book is well written, interesting, even funny at times, down to earth and informative. If you are the parent of a teenage daughter, you will miss a lot if you don't read it.

So buy it, read it, absorb it, and lose some of the gray ashen pallor which is the sure hallmark of the parent of a teenager.

Fitzhugh Dodson, Ph.D.

1
INTRODUCTION

A group of women are gathered in a local school. They are mothers whose daughters range in age from three to eighteen. You can easily spot the mothers* of the teenage girls. They look worn, weary and worried. *This need not be you.* You can learn to enjoy your teenage daughter. This book will show you how. It will explain how not to over- or underreact to your daughter's typically outlandish adolescent behavior. It will show you when and how to loosen the reins.

The purpose of this book is to help you enjoy your daughter as she is—not as you would like her to be. It is not an attempt to change either of you; instead the goal is to change habitual negative reactions into positive ones. The book suggests thoughtful, honest and loving responses to typical teenage behavior. (Let the psychologists explain the "whys" of such behavior.) At first glance, you may feel that the suggested responses are too permissive. However, if you read carefully you will find that it is never suggested that you allow your daughter to *do* whatever she

---

* The suggested responses and attitudes are also appropriate for a father or any person in the custodial role, since typical adolescent behavior is directed primarily at the person who has provided emotional security and protection during the child's early years. The adolescent needs to separate from that person, and in order for her to effect the separation, the parent-child confrontations will be similar whether the authority figure is male or female, parent or guardian.

wants, *only to think and feel as she wishes*. Suggestions are even made as to when and how to guide your daughter's words and choice of dress. What the book does encourage is that you reserve your *No's* for only those things which affect your daughter's safety and overall well-being, or for certain aspects of her behavior which you find particularly annoying.

The issues discussed here apply to females between the ages of ten and twenty. Since individual development from girlhood to womanhood varies so greatly, with a few exceptions specific ages are not indicated. However, most girls will exhibit most of the described behavior sometime during their second decade of life.

Sometimes our "high-tech" society extends adolescence even longer than anyone anticipated. One mother recently reported that her twenty-six-year-old daughter (who was a medical resident) still behaved like an adolescent. It seems the time and energy spent by both of them in getting the daughter into and through medical school had left little over for the daughter's emotional development.

The subject of the book is your daughter; however, the focus is on you. Many mothers today are unable to share their concerns about their daughters because of physical separation from their families and their roots, or because they or their contemporaries are too busy working. As a result, there is a feeling of isolation and uncertainty about the "right" way to bring up adolescents. Be assured that there is no "right" way—only a way that is right for you and your daughter. Also be assured that your daughter is not abnormal even if she has *never* spoken a civil word to her sister or treats you with disdain (at best).

Remember, you and your daughter are separate people. You may be very different or very similar, but you are separate. Adolescence is a time for your daughter to find out who she is and how to live a life that is best for her. It is not the time for a test of wills or the time for you to try to change your daughter into a different person. Instead, relax, be honest, and enjoy the emerging adult.

2
HOPED-FOR MIRACLES

- She will voluntarily lower the television when you have a headache.

- She will walk with you even though you are wearing jogging shorts.

- She will buy flowers for *your* luncheon guests.

- She will volunteer to shop for a sick neighbor.

- She will take over her brother's paper route without being asked so he can train for the marathon.

- She will write to her grandparents while she's at camp; she will even write *you* a letter.

- She will ask for your advice and follow it.

- She will stop putting empty milk cartons back in the refrigerator.

- She will buy you a present with her first paycheck.

- She will stop buying records.

- She will remember that you are having guests for dinner and the living room will be clean when you come home.

- She will finally decide what to wear.
- She will write a letter to the editor.
- She will let you have the last word.

With a little humor and a lot of patience and understanding, these can be everyday occurrences, not miracles. It isn't easy . . . but it is possible. Read on.

3
HER BEHAVIOR

ATTITUDE

INSOLENCE

You don't know which is worse—your daughter's whining when she was three or her contemptuous attitude of today. *You just can't do anything right! Accept it!* Your daughter is not rejecting your values and teachings; she is just testing them out herself so that when she adopts them, she will feel they are her own ideas and values, not yours. In the process she alternates among being rude, obnoxious, condescending and contemptuous toward you. You may even be told you "disgust" her. You are also accused of being dishonest (once you sampled a cherry from the supermarket fruit bin), ignorant (you don't remember the name of the first astronaut on the moon), selfish (you finally replaced your threadbare winter coat with a new one), lazy (you have someone come in to wash the windows), unfeeling (you still buy white tuna fish) and a phony (you had dinner with a boss you dislike).

React to your daughter's actions, however, not to her words. Most of the time she does what she has been taught to do, not what she says. She may answer your every comment, your every request, no matter how innocuous, with an impudent remark—but remember, she does the dishes without being asked when you work late.

Generally, it is best to ignore your daughter's insolence unless she does or says something that is particularly offensive to you. If, for example, she uses foul language in your presence, explain that you don't like to hear such talk. Tell her that if she feels she must speak that way, to please do so where you cannot hear her.

Count to ten (more than once, if necessary) when you ask your daughter, "How did your day go, dear?" and she responds with a look that would shrivel the Jolly Green Giant. *How dare you speak to her!* Even though you feel like wringing her neck, don't. And you cannot respond to her look with concern and say "I guess it wasn't too good," because she will accuse you of prying. You can't completely ignore her, either, because she will use that against you later and claim you don't care about her. The best response to her glare is to let it pass and chat about your day instead. After the tension of the moment wanes and she realizes you are not going to play Twenty Questions, she may want to talk.

Don't take your daughter's insolent looks or remarks as a personal rebuff. If you do, you will set up a no-win situation between the two of you that will persist throughout your relationship. Neither of you will ever get beyond her insolence and you will never find out about her day. Even if your daughter's response to your first question was "What the hell [or worse] do you care?" simply say that you *do* care and then talk about something else. If you respond in a positive manner (as long as your patience holds up), she will get the right message. If, instead, you react as she acts, you are in effect sanctioning her rude and disrespectful behavior.

Remember, too, that your daughter probably behaves much more nicely to others than she does to you. Some teacher friends have observed that adolescent girls exhibit insolent behavior at home *or* at school *or* on the streets. It may be more pleasant for you if your daughter is well behaved at home, but it is far more important in terms of her personal safety and future success that she not be a smart aleck in the street or a wise guy at school. Allow your daughter her mini-rebellions. Otherwise, you run the risk of crushing her spirit or forcing her to separate herself from

you when you are not even around—and where it is more dangerous for her to do so.

MISS KNOW-IT-ALL

Once you accept the fact that you "don't know anything about
anything," life will run a lot more smoothly. What it boils down to
is being adult enough to let your daughter have the last word.
Your daughter is embarrassed when she's wrong. She views the
correction of her comments as a criticism of her entire self. However, you as an adult, are able to be contradicted without your
ego being involved.

As your daughter gains more confidence in herself, she will
contradict you less often. But for now, if you tell a story in her
presence about when she was four months old and wearing a pink
diaper, and she corrects you by saying that the diaper was green,
let the diaper be green. It's useless to explain that since she was
only four months old at the time, she couldn't possibly know the
color of her diaper. Remember, she is not correcting you to be
obstinate or rude; she really believes that she is right. (Maybe
you told the story ten years ago and you said then that the diaper
was green.) You can correct her manners later and *in private* by
reminding her that it is rude to interrupt and also that it is embarrassing to you to have her constantly correct you—people will
think you have brought her up without any manners! This way,
you are not taking issue with what she believes, only with how or
where she expresses her beliefs.

PRONOUNCEMENTS

Your daughter doesn't mean to be disrespectful. She is just very
frightened about crossing the bridge between childhood and
adulthood, and you are the most likely person upon whom she can
test what she perceives to be adult rights and privileges. Therefore, she "announces." *She is going* to the 10:00 p.m. movie; *she
is getting* her nose pierced; *she is not going* to school tomorrow;
she is moving to Australia after graduation.

For the most part, it is best to ignore such pronouncements.

The outlandish ones will never come to pass and the others are relatively harmless. For example, my daughter "announced" a planned evening excursion with three of her friends to a tawdry amusement park. (Over my dead body, I thought.) However, rather than react to something that was highly unlikely to occur since the four of them pledged only to go together and they had never yet all been able to get together for anything, I held my tongue. Besides, they probably didn't really want to go. Otherwise, they would not have been so insistent about needing to go as a foursome. The girls knew the area was seedy and unsafe. All they really wanted to do was to assert themselves. As long as they were allowed the right to do so through a verbal effort, there was no need for a confrontation.

The following year the same girls "announced" they were going to get summer jobs as waitresses in a swank resort town and share an apartment. This time, since there was no joint pact, I decided some intervention on my part was necessary. Rather than point out all the dangers that could befall a group of sixteen-year-old girls living on their own, I suggested they find out about available apartments in the area. The rentals quoted quickly squashed their idea. However, my daughter did not lose face and we did not need to exchange harsh words about something that had practically a zero chance of taking place.

If your daughter is allowed to freely express her thoughts and ideas, she will not need to act them out physically. She needs to know she is her own person. If you react with patience and tact, and cross the bridges when you come to them, it will not be necessary for your daughter to do something foolish in order to separate herself from you. She just needs to feel free to be free.

SWEETNESS AND LIGHT

This phase usually occurs twice—once at the beginning of adolescence, and again shortly after the insolent phase.

The first phase manifests itself sometime around sixth grade. Your daughter is content to talk to you, read, daydream or watch television. Between periods of lazing on the couch and petting the puppy, she offers to help with dinner and the dishes. She's thoughtful, considerate and kind. She brings you coffee, she folds the laundry, she converses politely with your friends. Don't congratulate yourself. You're not going to miss the teenage turmoil. This is merely the calm before the storm.

The second angelic phase often occurs sometime during your daughter's junior or senior high-school year. She is *sooo* polite to you—she even speaks civilly to her brothers and sisters. She is constantly offering to help you. She calls to let you know she'll be ten minutes late. She asks you about your day. She's so sweet you may have to watch your sugar level. Don't worry, she's not trying to hide anything. She is just gathering energy for her next storm. At fourteen she was frenetic about pimples; at eighteen she may become equally frenetic about philosophy.

SHE DOESN'T LIKE YOU

While it is not pleasant to have your daughter not like you, she does have that right. She should be as respectful and considerate of you as she would be toward any person, but you cannot force her to think you're terrific. Look at it from her point of view. She is entering a world where people look, feel, think and act differently, and she finds you lacking.

It hurts. For several years she depended on you for her existence and happiness. You were her best friend. You took her places and baked cookies together. You took care of her when she was sick and gave her money for ice cream. Now, all of a sudden, it seems you have become a stupid, repulsive person. She takes your every flaw and magnifies it. You are no longer her beautiful, well-dressed "Mommy" but wrinkled and hopelessly old-fashioned. You are no longer a good neighbor but a gossip. You're revolting—you snort and snore. You're a failure—you have yet to sell a painting or become financially successful. You're a bore and your friends are even worse. In short, she realizes you are not the superstar she once thought you were.

Before, all you had to be was her mother. Now, even if you were Superwoman, you still wouldn't be good enough. You may be a perfect person or have just made your first million—you will still be inadequate in your daughter's eyes.

Recognize that it is not abnormal for her to feel this way. This is just another one of her ways of putting space between you.

However, let her know loudly and clearly that you still deserve to be treated with respect simply because you are a human being, whether or not she "approves" of you. Don't try to make her like you or feel guilty for not doing so. Don't defend yourself—you don't need to. Just ride it through . . . but you must make sure your daughter understands that while she has the right not to like you, she should not turn her dissatisfaction with you inward. For example, explain that she shouldn't smoke to spite you—she will only hurt herself. Ditto for getting pregnant or dropping out of school or not attending college. Make it clear to her that if she has problems with you, it is better to let the relationship suffer or be put on the shelf for a while rather than for her to take out her disappointment in you on herself. Make sure she realizes that your primary concern is how she views herself, not how she views you.

REBELLIOUSNESS

A certain amount of rebellious behavior has always been accepted of boys—but not of girls. Teenage boys are encouraged to learn from experience, yet society often denies such opportunities to girls. Parents get less excited about their teenage son who got caught skinny-dipping in the local reservoir or was discovered drunk in the family den than they would if their teenage daughter had behaved in the same way. Some parents may even brag about the mischief their sons get into or about their sexual prowess, yet will be shocked by anything similar that their daughter does.

Your daughter has as much a right to make her own mistakes as does your son. Sometimes she may seem overzealous in her efforts, but remember, the tighter you hold the reins, the more she will struggle to be free. Don't force her to break the reins completely in order to assert herself. Loosen up gradually but steadily. Give her the opportunity to learn to control herself.

Also, don't think you are not a controlling parent just because you are not strict. You may let your daughter do and try a lot of things, but you may still be controlling her by doing too much for her. Let her learn to take care of herself. If her button falls off, let her sew it on. Don't always say, "You look very nice dear, but wouldn't lower heels be more appropriate?'' If she has a problem with one of her teachers, let her try to work it out. Don't always run interference for her. If she drove into a neighbor's flower bed, don't make the restitution for her; let her do it. Don't tell her not to worry about writing away for college applications—that you will do it for her. In short, don't smother her.

Give your daughter the opportunity to be wrong, to fail, to worry . . . to be in charge of her life. Encourage her to participate in decisions which affect not only her but the whole family. Let her learn to express herself and be assertive even when her beliefs or ways of doing things are contrary to yours.

It is important not to squash your daughter's rebelliousness. Many young women growing up today will work outside their homes whether or not they marry or have children. Your daughter needs to learn to stand up for herself and discover who she is. Many women are underachievers because they were never allowed or encouraged to ''go for it.'' Let your daughter know she has rights. If you always need to win or be in control, she will either break away completely so her self can survive, or she will bend to you and never learn to be her own person.

AFFLICTIONS

ABSENTMINDEDNESS

If your daughter is not tripping over her clogs, it is only because she cannot find them. Nowadays, she cannot find anything. Bus passes and keys get lost. School assignments mysteriously disappear. Lunches and school books get left at home.

I know a teenage girl who reached her first-period class before she realized that she had left her book-bag at home. One forgotten book I could understand, but I still cannot fathom how someone who usually walks almost a mile with a twenty-pound pack on her back would not miss it—but then I'm not a teenager.

During this phase your daughter also has a complete block with respect to anything you asked her to do. Actually, the only thing she can remember your saying to her is that you would increase her allowance.

As with much of your daughter's adolescent behavior, the only remedy to this phase is time . . . and a spare set of keys.

BEING FOURTEEN

No matter what your daughter's personality or rate of development, at some point she will be Fourteen. Being Fourteen is not a chronological point but a unique phase in your daughter's development. At Fourteen she typically resembles an oversize child and shows no indication that she will become a graceful young woman.

You feel your home has been invaded by a new species. Everything your daughter does is exaggerated. If she was messy before, now you can never walk in the kitchen without your feet sticking to the floor. If she liked to talk on the phone before, it is now permanently attached to her ear. If she tended to be a little lazy before, she now never rises before noon on the weekends. If she liked to chew gum before, she now chews whole packs at a time. (If her orthodontist complains, she will think twice about chewing a wad of gum again; but all she will do is *think* twice. The mouth will soon be chewing once more.) She is around even when she isn't. She forgets to turn off her light or stereo. Pieces of gum wrappers mark her trail. Smells of spilled nail polish remover and too much perfume permeate the house. Don't fret. She will soon be fifteen. Just open the windows (but don't jump).

"SOAPS"

Nowadays, your daughter's interest is directed at just about anything that wastes time. She is totally engrossed in her favorite television show or a Rubik's cube or is plugged into her earphones. Very few teens do not display this kind of compulsiveness, and fewer still direct it toward something constructive like studying. For the most part, however, the time your daughter spends in front of the television is restricted to what is "in" at the time. A while ago, *General Hospital* was a must for all teenagers, both male and female.

As with most things your teenage daughter does, her involvement is total. She will rush home or hang up the phone so as not to miss a single second of the "in" show. I remember sitting for hours with my friends playing canasta, while our mothers badgered us about the beautiful weather outside. We, however, never altered our daily routine of rushing home, dropping off our books and running to Sue's house for three solid hours of cards before dinner. I think this lasted until we discovered boys. Obviously, it was impossible for them to discover us since we never ventured out.

Teens don't change, only the focus of interest does. One year it may be *General Hospital,* another year posters of the Rolling Stones or Bruce Springsteen records. As a parent you have a role to play. You must mention the starving children and your overdue rent upon sight of a new record or another poster. You must tell your daughter she will need bifocals by the time she is twenty if she does not unglue her eyes from the television. You must constantly remind her that there are such things as fresh air and blue sky. If you do not repeat these admonitions the requisite number of times, you will be accused of not caring. However, you must not take yourself too seriously.

In the meantime, rather than fight the inevitable, join it. Use the plots and characters of the "soaps" to get your own messages across. The programs deal with the tough issues of the day, such as drug and alcohol addiction, teen runaways, unwanted pregnancy, divorce and so on *ad nauseam*. The villains are eventually punished and the good guys win out. Listen to your daughter's comments about the "soaps." She may surprise you with her own sensible solutions to the difficulties presented; or you may discover she is on the wrong track about a particular subject. It will be easier to set her straight by discussing what Luke or Laura (of *General Hospital*) should do than by lecturing her about what she should or should not do. Also, the myriad problems presented on these shows give you an opportunity to discuss topics which you may have felt uncomfortable about bringing up, or which had not occurred to you.

Let your daughter's compulsive behavior run its natural course. Soon the records will gather dust, Dr. Drake will be replaced by the boy next door, and the dollars will be spent on something more worthwhile—like eye shadow.

TELEPHONITIS

Despite your daughter's addiction to the soaps, you probably aren't ready to throw the television out the window—more likely you want to rip the telephone off the wall. It seems the only time it's not ringing is when she is already using it. You have tried reason, logic, threats and punishment, and nothing works. Nothing will. That doesn't mean you should cease trying. As a parent you are supposed to nag. Otherwise your daughter will feel neglected and your not nagging will justify umpteen hours of telephone talk about how you don't care about her.

Typically, your daughter and her friends will call each other every evening to discuss the events of the day, their homework and what to wear the next day. Each topic necessitates a separate call to each friend. There seems to be some unwritten rule of teen telephone etiquette that more than one topic cannot be discussed during the same telephone call. Also, today's teen telephone etiquette allows a home version of the office telephone power play. The less popular caller holds on while the more popular girl fixes herself a snack or finishes polishing her nails.

Your daughter has at least one friend who has no telephone manners. She always calls when everyone is asleep. No matter that *you* have told Irene not to call after 10:00 p.m. or before 10:00 a.m. on weekends, when the telephone rings at odd times, if it is not your mother, it is Irene. (Irene has the problem . . . don't take it out on your daughter. And while it is annoying, it is probably not worth talking to Irene's family about. Keep trying to get through to Irene.)

Then there is your other daughter. Her telephoning is done in the wee hours of the morning. When I went to school, my friends and I would meet every day at the same time and at the same place. Today, however, because of sleepovers, traveling parents, divorce and joint custody agreements, where a teen will sleep on a particular night is not always known in advance. Therefore, arrangements about when and where to meet are made on a daily basis. For example, after school Carol and my daughter agree to meet on a certain corner at 7:30 a.m. and walk to school together. However, Carol is not sure whether her stepmother will remember to wake her up, and her alarm clock is broken. My daughter agrees to "ring" her twice at 6:30 a.m. to wake her up. The next morning I hear my daughter's alarms (she sets two just in case one doesn't work) go off at 6:15 a.m.—she needs to be sure she will be awake enough to make a phone call. Promptly at 6:30 a.m. I hear the telephone being dialed as she rings Carol. However, our telephone soon rings. It's Carol wanting to know whether that was my daughter ringing because she wasn't sure . . . and so my day begins as my last one ended—with ringing in my ears.

Of course the hours that your daughter spends talking on the telephone are a tremendous waste of time. She should be doing something constructive like reading or practicing the piano or cleaning her room. However, I have no counterargument to my daughter's contention that I should be happy she is at home and not out. Would I rather she be in some lovers' lane or game arcade, or home, safe and snug, talking on the telephone? Besides, says she, if it wasn't the telephone, she would be watching television or listening to records. "So what's the difference?"

The difference of course is the telephone bill. Parents have attempted all types of systems to limit teenage telephone use—installing locks, having a dime jar, limiting the hours when calls can be received or made, having the teen pay a percentage of the bill. However, nothing works. You need to make an important call and cannot find the key to the lock; your daughter's sick friend calls for school assignments during the off-limits hours; or your daughter is more than willing to pay a portion of the bill (providing, of course, you increase her allowance).

Another problem is your getting through to home. For example, if you work and want to call your daughter to let her know you will be late, it's impossible. You need to call a neighbor to go over and ask your daughter to get off the telephone.

My daughter suggested that her own telephone line would be the only solution. I always strongly objected even though she said she would pay for it, because I believe two phone lines for a family of three is an unnecessary extravagance. Anyhow, I practically never use the telephone at home and I don't own any telephone company stock. Besides, I could foresee my daughter receiving calls on my line and making calls on hers (or more likely, the other way around). Eventually I gave in and agreed to allow her to get her own telephone number . . . on the condition that my telephone would be removed and the few times I needed to make a call I would use hers and reimburse her. She was appalled at this idea. *I was right*—all she wanted was one line for incoming calls and another for outgoing calls.

Telephonitis is a disease that strikes almost all teenage girls. The only cure is time. The earlier in life the disease strikes, the more severe it is and the longer it will last. If your daughter has not succumbed to telephonitis during her high-school years, don't rejoice prematurely. It will strike while she is away at college, and then she will only know how to call collect.

VIDEO GAMES

There has been a lot of talk about teenagers wasting money and time at video arcades. Life would be wonderful if we could close down the time wasters and make sure our children did something constructive instead. However, be realistic. So they're spending lunch money. My guess is they are buying pizza and skipping the Coke and ice cream. So they're wasting time. Most likely if they weren't in the arcade, they'd be talking on the telephone, listening to records or watching television. Sure the video parlors are a waste of time and money, but so are most things a teenager buys and does. At least in a video parlor, if your daughter feels a need to "hang out," she is doing it in a somewhat protected environment.

This might be a good time, though, to talk about a part-time job or to sign your daughter up for those drum lessons she always wanted. Also consider paying her to do some of the work which you normally do, as long as she agrees to do it on a regular and consistent basis—for example, mowing the lawn or doing the marketing. Don't hound her about how she is wasting her life without providing an alternative. Like most teens she's compulsive. Sometimes it's the telephone, sometimes it's her hair, and now it's video games. The compulsion will spend itself eventually, but remember, there are two compulsions at work with video games—your daughter's natural compulsive behavior and the "one-potato-chip" syndrome. Once begun, it's hard for anyone, adults included, to resist "one more try."

INSECURITIES

TIMIDITY

You want your daughter to feel confident and assertive enough to withstand peer pressure, debate a teacher, ask for a job. Accepting your daughter for who she is and recognizing her as her own person is one part of confidence-building. Another is allowing her to have the experience of exercising some control over her life. Give your daughter the opportunity to know that she is a responsible person. Let her learn from experience, even if the experience sometimes results in failure.

Perhaps you can arrange for your daughter to travel, by herself, to visit a friend or relative in another state. True, she may get lost or lose her ticket, but she must have the opportunity to have a problem, to be afraid, and to be able to solve it herself. For example, a twelve-year-old girl I know was invited to spend a day at an elite private school located in the outskirts of a large city. She took the school's bus there and was to return home by special car service. While at work the mother received a message: "I missed the cab. Don't worry." Naturally the mother wasn't worried, she was frantic . . . it was the middle of January, it was 5:00 p.m. and already dark and snowy, and her daughter was on empty school grounds in the middle of nowhere! Fortunately the girl arrived home before the mother called the National Guard. The mother thought her daughter would be upset. Instead the girl was exhilarated. She told her mother she *was* afraid but she "whistled a happy tune." *The girl was frightened but she took care of the situation.* She had waited an hour for the car service and finally realized she was on the wrong street. She went back into the empty school building and found a telephone and called the car service again, explaining what had happened. This time the service knew exactly where to pick her up. She'd thought to call her mother and let her know she'd be home late. Perhaps another child would not have waited an hour. However, knowing first-hand that she could handle a frightening situation gave the girl more confidence than could any of her mother's words.

Encourage your daughter to experience being in a position of authority or in a situation where she stands on her own merits. Suggest babysitting, working as a camp counselor, volunteer work, teaching Sunday school, a part-time job. Remember, you probably boss her around at home, her teachers are always telling her what to do, her father teases her. All that can make your daughter's self-confidence pretty thin. Give her some responsibility at home. Let her *do* the laundry, not just help you. Take the chance of her not sorting the clothes properly and having a red shirt run all over the white socks. (If she did this to spite you or to get out of doing any work, read this book twice.)

Don't make your daughter feel she is incapable of doing a job from beginning to end. Don't intervene in the middle or redo what she has done because you can do it better. Encourage her to try new things and expose her to as many positive experiences as possible. Set an example for her by letting her know that at times you lack confidence too, but that you don't let your uncertainty prevent you from trying. For example, you are planning to run for the local school board and your daughter asks if you feel you will be elected. You respond "probably not" and she wants to know why then you are spending all your free time making posters and giving speeches. You explain that even though you have many doubts about your chances of winning and tremble when speaking in front of a group, one thing you know for certain—if you didn't run, you would never be elected. Tell your daughter that if she wants something, she should not be afraid to try for it. For example, if she got a B on her history paper and she thinks she deserves an A, she has nothing to lose by asking the teacher to reread her paper. Even if her voice squeaks when asking, the important thing is that she ask. At worst, the teacher will say no. At best, she will receive her A.

Also, much of your daughter's confidence depends on her appearance. While the majority of girls develop into at least passably attractive young women, it is often difficult for your daughter to believe that, even though you know it to be true.

Luck and creativity are helpful. I know of two sisters, one of whom was more attractive than the other. One recent Halloween the plainer girl dressed as a "lady of the evening." She looked gorgeous. Nobody (except maybe her mother) could believe it. That girl got so much confidence from knowing that she'd be pretty when she grew up. That knowledge helped her move out from her sister's shadow and become her own person. She was so much more confident of herself that she started doing better in school and making her own friends.

An opportunity to dress up can really build your daughter's self-assurance. I remember when my daughter tried on one of my office dresses. At that time she was pudgy and the dress alone did nothing for her. However, when we added stockings and high heels and a little makeup, she looked so good we decided to go out to dinner to show her off. Taking a look into her future and knowing she would turn out okay helped her handle her pimples and baby fat.

Sometimes, though, your daughter is in a real rut with respect to how she looks, and nothing seems to work. All her friends look terrific except her. Remind her that those who blossom first also fade first. You could tell her how lucky she is, because the longer it takes for her to flower, the longer her flower will last. After I told this to my daughter, I heard her talking on the phone to one of her girl friends. They were congratulating themselves on their respective luck in being plain. Great sympathy was being expressed for their less fortunate pretty friends.

FEARFULNESS

GENERAL. Young teens are full of fears ... fear of crowds, of high places, of snakes, of their parents dying. These will come and go in varying intensity depending on your daughter's personality and the "in" fear of the day—germ warfare, Son of Sam, mercury-poisoned fish. Don't be alarmed if she refuses to go in the kitchen before another family member checks it out for bugs. She is as extreme about her fear of bugs as she is about anything else she likes or dislikes.

Sometimes fear can be funny. Not too long ago we were invaded by a pair of giant water bugs. We all shrieked and giggled like ten-year-olds during the attack. Nobody was brave enough to step on them and hear the crunch of their shells. Instead, we armed ourselves with cardboard and broom handles. We were able to effect their retreat to the kitchen sink where we drowned them. Using an entire roll of paper towels we buried them in the garbage. Here we were, one adult and two nearly so, having a grand time with our fear.

If your daughter changes fears often and has a sense of humor about them, you need not be concerned. However, a fear that she holds on to and that interferes with how she lives is cause for concern. Perhaps you are coming home with too many horror stories about street crime and are at the same time overprotective, not letting her walk home the two blocks from her friend's house even though it may be only 9:00 p.m. True, there are some neighborhoods where your daughter would need to be escorted home, but if it is safe for you, it should be safe for her. If your fear is unrealistic, don't be surprised if your daughter distorts it to the point where she will not go anywhere by herself at night, even if it is just across the street. Children often misinterpret their parents' fears. If you are obsessed about telling her never to open the door to strangers, don't be surprised if she insists on locks for her windows even if her room is on the twelfth floor. If you treat every scratch as a major wound, don't be surprised if she is afraid of crowds for fear of catching an infection.

Be honest with yourself and see if perhaps you are trying to control your daughter through her fears. It is one thing to keep a two-year-old fearful of a hot stove; it's another to keep a teen indoors because she's afraid to go out. (Besides, this will backfire on you, because you will wind up being the one controlled. *You* will have to stay in with her because she will make you feel so guilty when you go out and leave her. If you do overcome your guilt and go out, she will get herself into a mess at home— perhaps she will make long-distance calls to everyone she knows, or she and a friend will drink themselves into a stupor— just so you won't go out again.)

There are, of course, some fears which we all have at one time or another. Will I be alone when my parents die? Will I pass my exams? Will I make a good impression? Will I ever have a boyfriend? Will anyone love me? Will I be able to get a job? And, if I do, will I be able to do it? Will I be alone in my old age? If your daughter seems concerned about these things, explain that everyone worries about them too. No one is totally free from concern about what others think, or never doubts their own ability, or never wonders whether they will be able to cope with difficult situations. Explain that if she allows herself to recognize her fear she will be able to overcome it. She may want to ease out of it or meet it head-on. If, for example, she is fearful of going for a summer job interview, perhaps she can go with a friend the first few times. She doesn't need to act like a pro the first time she does something.

If she is worried about doing a somersault in gym because she is overweight and the others will laugh, explain that her weight is no secret. She probably will look funny, but so what. Tell her about the time your date took you to a crowded restaurant and you dipped the shrimp in the tea instead of the hot sauce and said loudly that the sauce was too mild. Or what about your first day at work when you were asked to photocopy a stack of papers. You took out all the staples and then the papers fell and scattered all over the floor. It took your boss an hour to resort them properly. Or remember when you complained to your best friend that she never got you a tennis game even though you always arranged games for her? She finally set up a doubles match and reserved the court for two hours but you couldn't hit the ball. It was center court, too, right in front of the club's grandstand. What about the time you froze at your class picnic because there was a very large insect on your knee? You refused to move for fear it was poisonous. It turned out to be a praying mantis (a benevolent grasshopper).

Your daughter needs to know that everyone gets laughed at sometimes. Sure you feel embarrassed at first, but soon you realize how funny you must have looked to everyone else and it becomes just as funny to you.

Let your daughter know it is normal to be afraid of making a fool of herself. However, she needs to understand that no matter how hard she tries not to have it happen, something will come up in her life when she is the butt of a joke. Doing a somersault in gym may be the first time she's laughed at, but it won't be the last. Depending on your daughter's personality, you might want to mention some of the "greats" who were laughed at in their time—those who thought the world round when everyone else thought it flat, the "fools" who explored the West or who discovered electricity or who persisted in teaching the mute to communicate. Ask her where the world would be today without them. Generally, this type of example is too abstract for a teen unless she has a particular interest onto which you can latch a "great." Perhaps if she is interested in being a pilot, you might mention the many who laughed at the Wright brothers.

If, however, after all your talk, your daughter is still overly fearful of attempting a somersault in front of her class, don't force her to. Let her stay home. Write the required excuse note. You want her to know that you are on her side and won't force her to make a fool of herself. As she grows more confident of herself overall, it will become easier for her to attempt things which she cannot do well or gracefully. In the meantime, give her as much moral support as you can. Let her know you love her. Encourage her to like herself well enough to lose weight. Help your daughter to gain confidence by expanding her horizons. Introduce her to new people and new places. Encourage her to participate in after-school activities and in community events.

Anxieties about exams, dating, love, loneliness, money, death are part of life. How *you* handle these will influence how your daughter copes with them. Show her that you are in control of the situation. If, for example, you are in a new neighborhood and miss having friends nearby, instead of staying home and complaining about being lonely, join a church or political group. If you are concerned about losing your job, show positive action by getting your resume ready or signing up for retraining courses. If you are concerned about losing your looks, start exercising regularly. Admitting your worries to your daughter and letting her know of your plans to allay your own anxieties will set an example for her to follow. You want to show her that she can control her own worries and fears and not let them control her.

DEATH. Death, like birth, is part of life. Everyone worries once in a while about when they are going to die and what it will be like. Today, teens face the idea of death almost every day. Television brings the dreadful realities of war and crime right into our living rooms, and in full color. Discuss death with your daughter.

Explain that while it happens to everyone, the odds are greatly in her favor that she will lead a full life and die of old age.

NUCLEAR WAR. Lately a great deal has been written concerning teens' fears of nuclear war. Notwithstanding the horror of a nuclear war, there is no reason to treat this fear differently than that of any other possible future catastrophe. Your daughter has probably said, ''Why bother studying [or something similar]? We're all going to be blown up soon anyway.'' Well, maybe we will and maybe we won't. However, the possibility that something awful *might* happen doesn't mean we should behave as if it already *had* happened. Explain to your daughter that it is one thing to plan for the future; it is another thing to live in it. She is here and alive today, and she should get the most out of the present.

Fears usually have a reasonable and logical basis, whether it is fear of a nuclear holocaust or strange situations or elevators. Most people are afraid of something, and your daughter's fears should not be made light of or classified as foolish. Instead, help her to come to grips with her fear and not let it intrude in her daily life. If it is a nuclear catastrophe she is feaful of, she can do two things: she can do something constructive and, for example, become involved in nuclear arms control or disarmament movements; or she can live with her cloud. (She may decide the latter, as pessimism is often a preferred teenage state.) What she cannot do, however, is let her fear dictate her life or use it as an excuse for not doing things.

CRIME. Don't be surprised if your daughter is not as fearful as you of city or suburban crime. She takes news of muggings and burglaries in stride. Even reports of heinous crimes such as the murder of a neighborhood teen do not affect her (unless it was someone she knew or knew of). As a matter of fact, a young adolescent gets a certain status from having observed a mugging or by living next to a house that was burglarized.

Your daughter is not hardhearted or unfeeling. She has just learned to adjust to today's horrors as the women of a century ago had to accept the possibility of dying in childbirth or the frequent loss of an infant. In other words, your daughter has learned to adapt to her environment. Of course you don't want her to be careless, but be happy that her instinct for survival is functioning well enough to enable her to live a normal life during an era of turbulent social change.

SCHOOL. If your daughter is afraid to go to school because of the violence there, check it out. If her fears are well founded, send her to another school, even if you have to move or get a second job to do so. If this is impossible, arrange a meeting with the school principal. Perhaps she can be switched from the classes where she has the greatest fear, or her schedule can be rearranged so she need not be one of the last ones on the stairways. If the principal balks ("If it's done for you, it will have to be done for the other parents"), explain that you're not the other parents; their children are their concern. Your concern is your daughter. She is afraid to go to school. You cannot arrange for her to go to another school. She is entitled to go to school. Legally, she has to go to school until she is sixteen. The school has a duty when it cares for your child to do so safely. Go higher than the principal, if necessary. Get help from your neighbors. If you make enough noise, you might get some action.

SELFISHNESS

Everyone in the household should have an opportunity to come first. However, if you have a teenage daughter she will feel that she *never* comes first. *Everyone* else gets what they want except her! Your explanation that life evens out in the long run will fall on deaf ears because as a teen, she is now-oriented and cannot or will not consider the future. You need to consider her period of intense selfishness as one in which she *needs,* not wants, to come first. This is extremely difficult. You may find it hard to even like her, let alone favor her, because of her selfishness. Further, a variation of Murphy's Law is probably working, and everything is wrong or out of kilter in the household. There may be illness, unemployment or whatever, but your daughter's only concern will be herself. She simply has no capacity for reason or empathy during this time.

You have a choice. You can either harangue her for her selfishness and get nowhere or help her through it by recognizing that her selfishness is simply the symptom of tremendous insecurity and fear. Right now, your daughter is not much different from the toddler who misbehaves most when the mother tells her she has a headache. The toddler is insecure because she knows she is dependent on the mother and she recognizes that her mother's illness is a threat to her own well-being. Your teen daughter is insecure because she realizes that soon she will have to depend on herself.

Extra effort is required to bolster your daughter even if you feel her need to be first is trivial in relation to other family needs. You probably disagree with me and think that catering to her quest for attention and concern for self in a time of someone else's *real* need is ridiculous. However, your daughter's present need for attention is just as real a need as an ill person's need for special care.

For example, a young teen girl I know was in the midst of her self-centered phase while her brother was seriously ill. The mother was also studying for the law boards at the same time. Objectively, the brother's need for care and the mother's need for time were greater than the daughter's concern about whether or not she would have the right shorts for camp. Wisely, though, the mother took time to take a good long look at her daughter. She realized she was a pretty pathetic creature. The "right" shorts were just a cover for her fears and insecurities. The young girl was going on a backpacking trip and she was worried. Would she be able to keep up? Would her pimples go away in time? Would the boys notice that she didn't swim on "certain" days? Would she get what her brother had? What if her brother died? Would it be her fault? Would her mother blame her? Those were just the surface worries . . . imagine what lay beneath! No wonder the girl had to focus on little things like the right shorts. The other worries were just too much for her to cope with at the time.

Look beyond your daughter's seemingly selfish behavior and understand what is triggering it. Find the time and energy to pay attention to her so she will feel like a worthy person and have the confidence to work out her own fears little by little. She needs reassurance that she has a right to exist. You can give her the little extra she needs in simple ways—by bringing home her favorite ice cream or magazine when you are exceptionally busy, or by taking time out to see a movie or get a haircut together. The sooner the phase is recognized and responded to, the sooner it will go away.

STINGINESS

Your daughter is exceedingly cheap. She thinks spending $5 on a gift is extravagant. She's not any more generous to herself. She shops only in secondhand clothing stores; she'll buy a used ten-speed; she'll tell you she'll make do with one bathing suit even though she is to be a swimming instructor at camp. Even her pencils are used until they are no more than two inches long.

You don't need to worry about this child spending a week's allowance on one eyeliner or finishing a quart of milk and a box of cookies at one time. You *are* worried, though, because all your friends' daughters are buying two of everything when they need only one, and are eating pints of ice cream and whole heads of lettuce at one sitting.

Relax, nothing is wrong with your daughter. If you look closely, you will see she is really as excessive as your friends' daughters. The only difference is that her compulsive excessiveness is stinginess while theirs is extravagance. If, however, the stinginess lingers after she has outgrown excessive behavior in other areas, it may be just her nature to be a tightwad, or it could be rooted in a lack of self-esteem. If she is only tight about spending money on others or always looks for bargains, she is entitled to be that way. If, however, she refuses to spend on things that interest her, she needs assistance in building up her feelings of self-worth. For example, if she loves to play her violin but refuses to spend money on rosin, or loves to go to the movies with her friends but now stays home because she "can't afford it," try to find out why she feels the need to deny herself pleasure. Perhaps she blames herself for your divorce or feels guilty about all the money her recent illness cost. Perhaps she is harboring a secret guilt, a thought or deed, and is afraid to tell you. If so, explain that everyone does things they wish they hadn't. Everyone has thoughts they are not proud of. Tell her she doesn't need to punish herself. Explain that adolescence is a time to learn from experience, and most likely she has learned not to do whatever it was again. (If you suspect serious wrongdoing, you have a duty to try to find out what it is and take appropriate action.)

Be gentle, especially if you suspect her guilt is based on some form of sexual behavior. A thirteen-year-old who has engaged in petting may think she has done the worst thing in the world. She hasn't, nor has the teen who has engaged in intercourse. If she's feeling so guilty, she knows not to be so free again. What you want to convey is your acceptance of her even when she's done ''a bad thing'' so she can accept herself. If she accepts herself, she will treat herself nicely and with respect. If she has no self-respect, she is more likely to repeat the undesired behavior.

STRANGENESS

LIFE ON A SMALL BED

Whether your family lives in three rooms or ten, chances are that your daughter lives on her bed. She sits on her bed to listen to the stereo, to do homework, to talk on the phone, to polish her nails. What makes the situation even worse is that the air pollution level is higher in her room than anywhere else because the window never gets opened and the door is always closed.

I was never able to displace my daughter from her private throne, but I was able to convince her to open the window when using nail polish remover. I was also able to secure her solemn oath that she would never strike a match in her room. Of course she insisted she never struck a match inside or outside the house because she *never* smoked *anything,* nor would she. I saw no point in getting sidetracked into a discussion about drugs since my concern was the horror that a spark could cause in a room filled with stuffed animals and records. My hope was that, should the situation arise where she felt ''compelled'' to try marijuana or a cigarette in the house (despite my other lectures), at least she would try it in a less flammable area.

THE RECLUSE

Your heretofore active and joyful daughter has become a recluse. She is content to stay at home and daydream and speak to her *one* friend occasionally. She is also very sweet to you, though secretive and uncommunicative. If you ask her what she is doing in her room behind closed doors, she will respond, "Nothing." Most likely she is right. Nothing is wrong and she is doing nothing.

Don't worry if she behaves this way. She is probably getting ready for a major change in her life—menstruation, a growth spurt (physical or emotional), the realization that someday she will be leaving home. She's just gathering her reserves to meet the upcoming challenge. There is not much you can do except realize that she's not behaving abnormally. I know it is annoying to see her just sitting there, doing nothing, "wasting her life." If it really irritates you, go to a movie.

You might find her willing to play Scrabble with you or to learn how to knit. Don't think she's peculiar if she does spend time with you when all your friends' teenage daughters won't even sit in the same room with them. Everyone has their own development schedule. If your daughter will do things with you, enjoy it, because she won't for long. Don't worry that you will become such a good friend that she won't do anything ever again with friends her own age. You might be a terrific person, but you are not that terrific. Just don't make her feel guilty about ignoring you when she emerges like a butterfly from a cocoon a few months later.

MANNERS

Your daughter has forgotten how to use a knife or chew with her mouth closed. It is often difficult for her to partake in even the most rudimentary elements of conversation. She grunts a "hello" to your guests and slams the door when she leaves. A short while ago she was ever so polite. She knew the difference between a salad fork and a regular fork. She offered to make you coffee when she went to the kitchen for a soda. Now, the French fry is eaten with her fingers at the dining room table, the napkin is used to wipe the ketchup off her knife, and plates are picked up to be licked clean of gravy.

You're horrified. The last time her table manners were this bad, she was nine months old. You berate her, asking where she learned to eat like that. All you get from her is that she *knows* what to do—but she's in her own home and she should be comfortable. You order her to leave the table, never to return. The scene is oft repeated over different offenses—her elbows are sprawled across the table or her legs rest on the opposite chair. Obviously, this is not the same daughter you raised with such patience and care. How are you going to be seen with her in public? You're all invited to your boss's house for dinner next week! Be prepared. One of two things will happen. She will either behave beautifully and you will be astonished, or she will tilt the chair back after dinner and belch. Just pray that your boss has teenagers too.

MAKEUP

Lately when you come home from work, or when your daughter arrives home, your hand automatically touches her forehead to check for fever. She has dark circles under her eyes and her cheeks are always flushed. Finally it dawns on you—the circles are from smudged eyeliner and the flush is from too much cheek blush.

You tell your daughter about the inadequacies of dime-store makeup and launch into a discussion about waterproof eye makeup and blendable blush. You even offer to take her shopping so she can buy what's best for her. Surprisingly, she eagerly agrees to go with you. It is only when you are writing a check for $37.90 to the department store that you realize you've been had.

CLOTHING

STYLE. Your daughter appears in the middle of the living room and asks, "How do I look?" How she actually looks is irrelevant, unless of course she's nude except for body tattoos or is wearing pierced earrings weighing at least five pounds each. The problem is how to answer. Your best response is "interesting" or "different" because she may be showing you the awful way Sally wears her hair. You will be in a lot of trouble if you answer, "Great!"

Your daughter will probably go through a period when she has absolutely no taste when it comes to her appearance. Some teens have a natural flair for choosing and wearing clothing and miss this awkward phase entirely. Your daughter, however, will want to wear clothing that is totally unbecoming to her. For example, at some point in puberty, pink is "in" and ruffles are everywhere, even if the teen wearing them is short and dumpy. Ribbons and barrettes (together) adorn the hair, often with a headband added. Turquoise is also popular, especially on those five feet and under and five ten and over. At the other extreme are girls who think even maroon is too bright, and the mere suggestion that they wear something "burgundy" is enough to keep them behind closed doors for days.

As awkwardness phases out, kinkiness phases in—barrettes lose ground to "punk" haircuts, jeans lose to purple miniskirts, ruffles give way to multifeathered earrings. Patience, humor and a little tongue-biting are the only remedies. Your daughter will learn to either lose weight or tone down her colors. She'll learn that green nail polish is not for her. The important thing now is not to destroy her confidence. It's how she thinks she looks that's important, and unless there is something terribly wrong with how she is dressed, it's best to let her learn in her own way.

APPROPRIATENESS. You may think summer begins on June 21. Actually, if you have a teenage daughter, it begins the day after summer clothes are purchased. It may be only March 20 and the wind's howl warns of a blizzard, but your daughter appears at the breakfast table in a gauze blouse and lemon-yellow cotton coveralls. You explain, "Sweetie, we're going to have a snowstorm. It's 25° outside now—you'll freeze." Her response, of course, is that she won't freeze because she will wear a sweater under her ski jacket. You next try playing on her vanity and mention how ridiculous and out of place she will look compared to all her friends who will still be dressed in wool and corduroy. She will promptly remind you how often you have told her not to do something just because her friends do. She has you trapped in your own argument. You could make a scene and get her to change clothes. But why? There really is no harm in her looking like a misplaced daffodil. Besides, this is *your* opportunity not to walk on the same side of the street with *her*. The only real solution to the problem is to wait until at least mid-May to buy summer clothes.

Sometimes a scene can be avoided if you choose your words carefully. For example, my daughter announced one icy January day that she was wearing clogs to school. She had a sixteen-block walk to school and several crowded stairways to negotiate between classes, but I was not up to a confrontation. Instead, I let money talk. Casually, I told her she could wear what she wanted but she would have to pay the medical costs of her broken leg, and quickly left the room. She went to school; the clogs stayed home.

Certain regions have peculiar teenage dress styles which have nothing to do with the weather. Often the peculiarities are very local and may affect students at only one school. One recent fall the local high-school girls attended classes sporting bare midriffs. My first reaction was that I would never let *my* daughter go to school dressed like that. Didn't those parents care how their daughters looked? However, I soon discovered two things. One, after a summer of viewing girls in bikinis, high-school boys are more interested in tossing a pigskin than they are in further tummy ogling; and two, by the time a parent would have won the battle, the war would have been over. Bare midriffs did not last because it hurt getting pinched by one's chemistry book.

As a parent you should certainly voice your opinion when you believe your daughter is dressed inappropriately. However, how adamant and strict you are in your actions should be based on real dangers, not merely differences of opinion between you and your daughter. For example, one extremely hot summer evening, my daughter was leaving the house wearing respectable-length shorts and a T-shirt. She was on her way to meet a friend and go to a movie. She mentioned she was meeting her friend on a downtown corner. I screeched, "You can't wait for anyone standing on a corner dressed like that!" She patiently reminded me that she was old enough to stand on a corner. I explained, "Yes . . . that's exactly why you can't stand on a corner . . . because you *are* old enough." She got the message and called her friend and made arrangements to meet inside the theater.

My reasonable concern about someone mistaking her for a teenage prostitute is worth a scene; the possibility that she may be ogled on the school bus is not. If you are selective about when to use your authority you will find you need to use it less. Also, you will be listened to more quickly and more often than if you constantly veto your daughter's actions.

Sometimes the way your daughter and her friends decide to dress can have amusing results. Several eighth-grade girls I know decided to dress as glamorous movie stars for a costume party. Out came hoop earrings and feather boas and nightgowns doubling as Jean Harlow evening gowns. On went eye shadow and false eyelashes and bright red nail polish. They left looking far too slinky and sexy for their years. It must have been an unusual party. The eighth-grade boys dressed as robots or pea shooters.

Also, don't be surprised if your daughter goes to the beach wearing jeans and a sweatshirt and heavy knee socks with sandals. She's covering up her budding breasts and hairy legs. In another summer or two, she will have learned to deal with her emerging sexuality and will appear on the beach in the skimpiest of bikinis. However, you, as her mother, are not supposed to know she has "emerged." She may brazenly parade along the shore or on the boardwalk but you will not be permitted to see how she looks in her new bikini.

PACKING

Today, our daughters go off to camp, to visit their fathers, to summer-study abroad, to grandma in Florida, to college. By the time your daughter is an adolescent, she will have her own philosophy about packing. She will want to go to summer camp or school either with an overnight bag or with a U-Haul.

Letting her pack exactly what she wants results in either pneumonia for her (rain slicker not taken to camp) or backache for you (squeezing trunks into the back seat of your two-door car and then carrying them up to her fourth-floor dorm room). I have not been permitted to participate in the actual packing since my daughter was eleven. You can, however, maintain a supervisory role through perseverence and ingenuity. You can make piles of camp-labeled clothes and hope they make it into the trunk. You can pack the rain slicker during the middle of the night or conveniently misplace half of your daughter's wardrobe. If she is one of those who takes all everywhere, your campaign must begin at the end of the preceding summer. You must get her to part with some of her stuffed animals and weed out her T-shirt collection. A Board of Health violation certificate is helpful. Also the threat of bedbugs is a good tactic, as most adolescent girls have an aversion to crawling things. In any event, even if you have succeeded in keeping her luggage physically manageable, you will be reminded by letter and by phone during the entire time she is away that she has nothing to wear and that everyone else packed twice as much.

Your success with the toothbrush-only type will not be much greater. Most likely, even if you manage to get her to pack the necessities, she will never look beyond the first level of the trunk or suitcase and will accuse you of not packing her shorts or a single towel. Your only reward will be very little laundry to do when she comes home.

4
YOUR ROLE

IN GENERAL

ACCEPTANCE

One day you decide you don't really like your daughter. You're not sure why ... all your friends think she is "such a lovely girl." They do not understand that when you see her sprawled on the couch, all you see is her mouth moving—either talking on the phone or chewing gum, or both. Nothing else moves. She has more rolls of fat on her body than you; or if she is thin, you are convinced her bones will snap from disuse. What has happened is that you have just realized that your daughter is not the superstar you thought she was. The A's stopped after grammar school; she did not make the varsity team; she will never have the chin to become a model. Your daughter is not any different than before but you have just discovered that she is who she is, not your idealized image. You're disappointed and it will take effort on your part to accept her for herself. Don't fault her for not being a star. Her uniqueness is enough to deserve your love and respect.

You also need to help your daughter accept her own limitations. If, for example, there is no hope that she will ever be a prima ballerina, don't behave as if you still expect her to be. (Of course, *she* can behave as if she still expects to get to the top.)

Let her know she can continue with her dancing lessons simply because she enjoys them. Let her know she need not always win or be the best to merit your approval. She has a right to some flaws. Love her, and help her to love herself, in spite of any of her failings or shortcomings.

COMMUNICATION

Communication need not be a "meaningful conversation." Communication is respect and understanding and sensing where your daughter "is at." Don't force it just because you think a mother is *supposed* to communicate with her daughter. The best way for you to communicate is by listening and observing. Keep in mind, too, that communication sometimes includes disagreement, but be sure after the smoke settles that your daughter is left with feelings of self-respect and self-worth.

If your daughter comes into the kitchen and sniffs the pots while you're cooking, chances are she has something to say. Don't pounce or she will clam up. Wait for her to begin. She'll probably start off with a cheery "Hi!" or a grumpy "Ugh!" about what you're preparing. In either case be attentive but continue with what you are doing and take your cue from her. If she then complains that her teacher is unfair, don't tell her he's entitled to a bad day too. Be on your daughter's side—at least at first. You can defend the teacher later, if necessary. Your best response would be "Oh," and to let her continue with her story. Try to see it from her point of view and acknowledge that she has a right to it. Then you can either support her view or not.

But, you say your daughter never talks to you! That's probably not true—she just never talks to you when you want to talk to her. Conversely, when she wants to talk to you, you are probably unavailable or unaware of her signals that she's ready to talk.

Your daughter may be the broadcaster type who delivers bulletins the minute you walk in the door: she got a 90 in her math test . . . her physics teacher is *soo* unfair . . . Andrea is in the hospital . . . her class is going to Washington, D.C., for a weekend . . . she's going on the Beverly Hills diet . . . you have to go to Parents' Night on Tuesday . . . all delivered in three seconds or less. But you really don't want to talk to her right now. You need to unwind and fix dinner. By the time you have changed your clothes and sat down it's too late to find out which Tuesday, which weekend, which hospital. She's busy with her homework or has gone to gymnastics. Later, after dinner and when you're ready to talk to her, she doesn't want to talk to you. By then it is all old news to her and the most you will get are monosyllabic answers to your questions.

Some teens have strange methods of communicating. All you need to do is be aware of them. For example, my daughter and I hadn't "communicated" for what seemed like ages. It wasn't until she started going to parties that we had a "meaningful" conversation. I waited up for her the first time she went out and discovered she loved to talk at night. Thereafter, I would always be up when she came home and we'd have a snack and talk for an hour or two about all kinds of things—her life, the world, my problems. One girl I know communicates with her mother indirectly. The girl has a telephone in her room but makes all her calls in the kitchen within easy hearing distance of her mother. She appears oblivious to her mother's eavesdropping. What she is really doing is letting her mother in on her life and trusting her mother to know when to interfere if something doesn't sound right. Your daughter may be sending out her own signals. Listen and look for them.

However, if you and she seem not to be communicating, step back and look at the situation objectively. Your daughter may be the type who likes to keep things to herself. (She is entitled to do that as long as it does not cause her physical or emotional distress.) Or, it may be that your interests are so far apart that you really have very little to say to her except to remind her to eat green vegetables. She may have even less to say to you. However, the fact that you may not be speaking "meaningfully" to each other does not mean there's no communication between you. You are communicating concern and love each time you ask her when she will be home or when you buy her favorite shampoo. She, too, is communicating love and respect when she offers to turn the radio down or clean the inside of the car. It's okay to keep in touch through everyday living. You need not feel the two of you must discuss Life. Besides, such discussions tend to be one-sided monologues given by you, with her only pretending to listen.

TOGETHERNESS

Togetherness can't be forced. It may be that you and your daughter have no common interests and, therefore, have no reason to spend any time together. However, with a little thought, you probably can find *something* your daughter will agree to do with you. For example, my daughter always enjoyed apartment hunting. Now when we both have nothing to do, we will take a walk and apartment hunt, pretending we are really going to move. She tells me how she would furnish the new apartment, and it is nice to hear her dreams. A friend's daughter likes to read. They often browse through bookstores together. Togetherness might even be the extraordinary moment when your daughter invites you to share her "Cinnamon Sin" lip gloss . . . you do it even if it stings!

Understand if your daughter doesn't want to go to a movie with you. After all, her friends might be there and if they see her there with you, they might think she had no one else to go with. That's also why she won't go shopping with you—unless you take her to the most expensive store in town. Try to respect your daughter's feelings about not being seen with you. If you really want her to accompany you somewhere, don't ask, "Why won't you go anywhere with me? Are you ashamed of me?" Instead, simply say you need her presence at a certain time, at a certain place, for a specific reason. She may surprise you and agree to have lunch with you and Aunt Helen so you can save face.

Naturally you would like your daughter to go bike riding with you or attend museum openings—both of which she finds equally distasteful. (The museum you can understand, but what's wrong with bike riding?) After all, you would like to do something with your daughter other than shopping with her at the local boutique. Here are some suggestions about how to be "together" with your daughter when she refuses to go anywhere with you. They may seem trivial but they epitomize what home and family are all about. Coupon clipping, pantry checking and meal planning can be shared activities. It is amazing how simple things can become a family ritual. Every Thursday night, after dinner, my daughter and I would sit down and prepare the shopping list. She even bought a coupon box for the house, and now she mails food coupons home from college. Also, all that advice to the working mother about cooking ahead can spoil a lot of togetherness. Take advantage of those rare evenings when no one has to rush off to a meeting or do lots of homework. It is fun to chop and stir-fry together. Setting the table, making the salad, fixing coffee, can be not chores but shared activities and a time to talk. Sunday mornings or weekday nights you can do the newspaper crossword puzzles or follow the stock market listings together.

Family occasions need not be special or expensive. Sometimes the unexpected or most humdrum activity can result in a memory of shared laughter. For example, one day my daughter, a child she was babysitting for, and I went to buy two small (or so I thought) camp trunks. Off to the store we went, made our purchase and left—me holding one trunk, and my daughter and her charge holding the other. After half a block, the little girl had to go to the bathroom. Hurriedly home they went and there I sat with the two trunks in the middle of a busy street awaiting rescue by a neighbor. My daughter gets hysterical with laughter every time she thinks of it. At least it wasn't raining.

What's important is the sharing, not the subject of the experience. Seize the moments as they come. Planned fun is never as good as when it is spontaneous. Be flexible enough to be aware of the potential of the moment and don't squash a good time by thinking that now that you are ''close,'' it's a good opportunity to deliver a lecture. If the two of you are having a great time while she's teaching you to roller-skate, don't bring up the subject of her going steady. It's unlikely anything you say at that time will change her feelings. All you will do is spoil the fun and wind up angry with her and yourself. A memory of a good time with you is more likely to get your daughter thinking about what you have said in the past than is a repeated lecture. So, if you and she are having fun together, enjoy the moment. Those times are rare and should be protected.

GIVING ADVICE

The purpose of your advice is not to order your daughter to do your bidding but to guide her toward making a wise decision. If you give advice, *give it as advice, not as an order!* If you want to tell your daughter what to do and what not to do, by all means do so, but when you give advice, allow her the right to reject it. If she does not follow your advice and even if it was a mistake for her not to do so, do not accuse her of "disobeying" you. Remember, advice is for those instances where your daughter will need to make her own decisions. You give it to make her aware of problems or dangers that she may not be aware of.

It doesn't matter whether your words are "pearls of wisdom" or that you are permitted to utter them only between biology chapters or during *General Hospital* commercial breaks. However, if you repeat your usual "tried and true," your words will go unheeded. Therefore, it is better to say the unexpected. For example, if your daughter is going away to camp, don't give her a list of do's and don'ts. She has heard them all before (or something similar) and nothing you say will register. It will go in one ear and out the other. A remark such as "If you're going to do something wrong, do it because *you want to do it*, not because someone else wants you to" is far more likely to get her attention. Furthermore, the substance of the remark will make her focus on the fact that she is primarily responsible for herself, and it lets her know you have confidence in her judgment. What you want to do is to remind your daughter to be guided by the values she has learned and not succumb to peer pressure.

Even if your advice appears to fall on deaf ears, it may still be effective. Something of what you say will sink in sooner or later. Your daughter hears what you say even if she claims otherwise or walks out on you before you've delivered the punch line. Don't let her rude behavior sidetrack you into a lecture about slamming doors. Continue with your discussion about hitchhiking or contraception or whatever. But be careful not to give advice about every single facet of your daughter's life, or you will run the risk of being shut off completely. My daughter let me know I was too heavy into my advisor role by ordering me not to give her any more advice about anything. I told her it was my job as a parent to give advice and that nobody was insisting she follow it. She said, "I'm not stupid! Don't you think that if what you say makes sense, I'm going to follow it?" I asked, "Then, what's the problem?" She explained that she didn't want any advice because she wanted to figure things out for herself and make her own mistakes. It seemed we had come to an impasse. She had a need to be able to err and I a need to guide her. We solved the problem by agreeing that when I felt a need to advise, I could do so, but she was free to leave the room. Thereafter, my advice was spoken to a wall—hopefully, with her intently listening at the other side.

DISCIPLINE

NAGGING

Your daughter always accuses you of nagging. "Pick, pick, pick. That's all you do." She is probably right, but ignore her comments. You're entitled to nag, but you don't need to overdo it by picking on her about picking on you. Or you may be a "screamer." If your screaming is merely a brief temper tantrum and is not giving you high blood pressure, don't worry about it. But remember, if you scream at your daughter, she does have the right to scream back at you.

Most teens will take their parents' ill-delivered expressions of care and anger in stride, provided that what is said is constructive and not merely derogatory. Take more care with *what* you say than *how* you say it. For example, if you want your daughter to get more exercise, don't keep telling her she looks like a lump of lard; instead, nag about the healthful benefits of exercise. If your daughter never calls when she's going to be late, don't scream that she is thoughtless and inconsiderate; remind her instead how much better a simple phone call will make you feel. If your daughter's grades are poor, don't call her stupid; instead insist she spend more time studying or that she get a tutor.

If your daughter tunes you out, change your style of delivery. Perhaps you should whisper or update your vocabulary. True, adults who speak like teens do sound ridiculous, but doing so may get her attention.

WHEN TO SAY NO

One day you realize with a shock that you no longer make the decisions for your daughter; the decisions that affect her will be made by her. For example, your daughter announces that she *could* go to Nowhere, U.S.A., if she wanted to. Your mind tells you, yes, she could. She knows where to get the bus and she does have the money. However, instead of reacting as if she were leaving on the next bus, ask, "Why do you want to go to Nowhere? Why would anyone want to go to Nowhere?" She informs you that there is to be a rock concert in Nowhere's coliseum that she would like to attend. What do you do now? You don't want her to go. *She mustn't go.* It's too dangerous. However, if you had been listening carefully, you would have noticed that she did not ask to go, nor did she even say she was going. All she said was that she *could* go. So, why not agree with her and say, "Yes, you are quite capable of traveling to Nowhere," and see what happens next.

Most often when teens come up with outlandish ideas, they just want recognition and affirmation of their capabilities. You need not respond to what may occur in the future. You only need to respond to your daughter's initial remarks. Often the best response is a short "Oh" or "Ummm," no matter how off-base the pronouncement.

If she *asks* to do something outlandish or says that she *is going to,* before you automatically say no, ask yourself why you do not want her to do it. Do you want her not to go because it might be dangerous? Or because *you* don't like rock concerts? Or because you are worried about what your friends or neighbors would think if you let her go? Remember, your daughter has some sense. If it is dangerous for her to go to a particular rock concert, she probably doesn't really want to go. However, it may not actually be dangerous. Look objectively at all aspects of the contemplated trip. How far is it? How will she get there? Where is the arena in relation to the city? Whom is she going with? How much will it cost her? Does she want to spend her money on the trip instead of saving it for a car? You can forbid her to go, but if your grounds are unreasonable or dishonest, she may not ask the next time. Your goal is to get her to make decisions wisely, to consider all that is involved. You don't want her to say yes without thinking; therefore you shouldn't say no without a lot of thought, either.

Perhaps the trip may only *seem* dangerous. For example, during the late 1960s I was taking care of two teen sisters who had permission from their parents to attend a peace rally to be held in a city two hundred miles distant. They planned to drive there in a pickup truck with several friends, leaving at the crack of dawn and getting home by midnight. Personally, I thought the trip was dangerous and was very concerned about their safety. However, analyzing my feelings, I realized I was not worried about anything that the girls would do. They were good drivers and the group was not wild, just full of life and energy and anxious to express their views and participate in their world. My concern was that they might be hurt as innocent bystanders— Kent State being not too far from my mind. I was also concerned they might be picked up for drug use. My goodbye speech requested their solemn promise that they would eliminate all traces of marijuana and any related paraphernalia from themselves, their gear and their truck, and that they would not stand within viewing or smelling distance of any drugs. Of course they protested that they *never* smoked, that *nothing* was in the truck. I didn't let myself get sidetracked into a lecture about drug use in general. Instead, I focused on the danger of the moment and ignored their protests. I reiterated my fear that they would become involved in a riot and that if one occurred, the police would be more likely to go after drug users than nonusers. I explained to them that their parents had not spent innummerable hours of worry and energy on them for them to be locked up for ten years on a drug charge.

They didn't want to be in the midst of a riot or go to jail, either. They took my warnings seriously. They stayed at the fringes of the demonstration, but they were happy to have had the opportunity to express themselves by their presence.

If your "no" is based on reasons other than danger, be honest and tell your daughter what they are. Don't attempt to disguise something as dangerous when your concern is what your neighbors will think. You may have a selfish reason for not wanting your daughter to do something, and you are entitled to it. However, your daughter also has a right to be selfish sometimes too.

For example, my daughter refused to be shown off at my office. I was very annoyed at first but realized she had the right to make the decision either to go and please me or not to go. My daughter's decision to refuse was selfish, but so was my desire to show her off.

Also, your daughter may want you to say no. My daughter announced one snowy Saturday night that she was going to a party in a dangerous part of the city. I asked her how she planned on getting there, since it was snowing and it would be impossible to get a taxi. She said they were going by subway. *"Travel by subway in the middle of the night?!! No way . . . You can't go!"* I yelled and braced myself for a stiff argument. However, all she said was "okay" and called her friend to say her mother wouldn't let her go. I realized my daughter wasn't stupid—she didn't want to do anything as crazy as travel by subway to and from an unsafe and unknown neighborhood in the middle of the night. How much nicer, though, it is to blame Mother than to appear cautious to one's friends. Besides, the sympathy she received was worth an entire evening of telephone calls.

Remember, you will not be in on most of the decisions that your daughter will need to make from now on. You probably will not even be around when she needs to make them. Some of her decisions you will disapprove of and some will be harmful to her. However, you must always be honest and reasonable with her if you want the communication channels to stay open. Otherwise, if you say no too often and without reason, she will no longer come to you for permission. As long as she asks you, you have the opportunity to point out dangers and pitfalls that she may not have considered. Even if she seems to pay no heed to your argument, she *has* heard you and will remember what you said for the next time.

CLOUT

It is easier to have clout if you are the major breadwinner in your family or a working mother, but you can have clout if your job is that of a homemaker only. Clout is what you bring with you when you say no or lay down the law. Fathers, as the traditional breadwinners, have had clout for years, which is one of the reasons they are obeyed more readily than mothers. Society toots the horn of the "man of the house." Pictures of men in power are everywhere.

It's time mothers tooted their own horns. If you work outside the home, make the most of any "perks" you get. Do you receive any special discounts or tickets as a result of your job? Are you so important that your company sends you on a business trip (even if it is only to Nowayville)? Do you have an expense account or get taken out to lunch often? Do you work in a well-known building or office park? Is your boss someone famous? If you're a traditional homemaker, do your cookies win prizes? Are you a Brownie Scout leader or officer of the local parents' association? Have you won any awards for any of your hobbies? Do you sing in the church choir? Are you a member of the auxiliary police or fire department?

Whatever you do or get that is "extra," flaunt it. Don't trivialize your rewards or accomplishments. Be proud of yourself and let your daughter know you are. You are proud of her achievements; let her be proud of yours. If you handle it right and believe in yourself, you will find that your daughter is respectful of you and proud to be a woman.

SPOILING HER

If you take the time and energy to discipline your daughter fairly, and if the limits you set have a reasonable basis, you will not spoil her. Giving her a little extra attention and thought is not spoiling her. Giving in to her because it is easier to say yes than no, is. Take the time to set limits and standards which are *for your daughter's benefit,* not for anyone else's. If you do set limits which are for your benefit or the benefit of others, say so and don't lamely disguise them as being anything else.

You should not deny your daughter something just because you feel it's for her own good to be denied something. It's fine not to buy an item because the family cannot afford it. However, there is no reason not to buy her special shampoo because "Who does she think she is asking me to spend $2.59 on a bottle of shampoo? She can use the store brand just like the rest of the family." *She thinks she is special and you should too.* Remember, if she feels she is valued by others, she will value herself. If she values herself, she will be able to resist the girl friend who asks her to shoplift, or to say no to a boy.

Feel free to satisfy your daughter's needs. You may think she needs three pairs of $15 jeans, but she may think she needs a $45 pair. Let her buy the expensive pair, as long as she understands that you can afford no more for jeans (and she is willing to wash the one pair often). Don't wheedle her down, claiming that if all she needs is one pair, she can have one $15 pair. She doesn't need one pair—*she needs one $45 pair*.

You need not worry about your daughter becoming spoiled if you treat her like a special person. For example, a family I know recently inherited some money. This family had gone through unusually difficult financial times and the parents decided to let each family member buy something from the inheritance that they felt they had been deprived of. The parents chose ordering-in Chinese food once a week; one son chose to resume his trumpet lessons; another child chose to visit a friend in another city. They all thought the teen girl would want her own stereo or expensive leather boots because she was very fond of "things" and spent all her money on clothes or tapes. She was also the type of teen who *needed* $50 running shoes (but would wear them until they fell apart) and would not shop anywhere but in expensive boutiques. Her choice? A popcorn maker! It seems that through the hard times, she had never felt deprived. She always got what she felt she needed. Her family had respected her expensive taste and she had respected the family budget by needing fewer things.

Wealth or lack of it is subjective. Some would consider anyone above the poverty line to be wealthy; others reserve that term only for the Rockefellers. My own definition is simple: anyone who has twice as much as I is wealthy. However, knowing what to give or how much to spend on teenagers is a universal problem regardless of one's position on the financial scale. For example, today prices for a pair of running shoes range from $10 to $100 + . Most of us can afford the $10 pair but very few can afford the truly expensive brands. However, just because you can afford $100 for a pair of shoes for your daughter, should you spend that much? Do you buy your daughter a fancy 12-speed bicycle? Or a car? Or, when she's older, a home? We all want our children to have their own resources and successes and to do for themselves, but at the same time we want them to have the best. The most reasonable approach is that if you can afford it *and* the object of the request is reasonable, why not enjoy your "wealth." If your daughter is a dedicated runner, why not buy the best shoe you can afford. Community standards should be considered as well. For example, a wealthy friend lives in an area where most high-school students have their own cars. The family can easily afford a new car for their daughter, so they need not worry about the temperament of a used car. However, it doesn't mean that the new car need be a BMW. Also, as my friend said, they will buy the car and keep it up because they can afford to, but that doesn't mean they will pay for their daughter's parking tickets.

Because of their wealth and the community standards, withholding a car from their daughter or making her pay for it so she could learn "responsibility" would be artificial. What may seem like an extravagance for one family may well be a necessity for another. If you can afford the "extravagant necessity," enjoy your good fortune. Denying it could easily destroy your credibility.

PUNISHMENT

Punishment is a tool which parents use in order to feel they are doing something, and to show the child that they care. However, it serves as little else. It doesn't get the room clean or the homework done on a regular basis. It doesn't change habits. All it really does is put an end to an immediate problem.

Sometimes you will feel the need to punish your daughter if she stays out too late by making her stay in the following weekend. However, if it becomes a pattern of one weekend out late and one weekend home, the punishment is obviously not effective. You need to work with your daughter so she will come home on time for her own safety and out of consideration for you. Your behavior and that of your daughter should be considered if you find yourself meting out punishment for the same "crime" over and over again. Does the punishment fit the crime? Is the punishment *wanted* because it is her way of getting your attention? Or because she cannot handle the situation for which she is being punished? Are your expectations unrealistic? Try to determine the cause of the problem that triggers the punishment.

If you find yourself punishing your daughter often for a variety of offenses, you are wasting your time. Punishment used sparingly will remind your daughter of what is expected of her but will only work as a sanction if she is controllable—either by you or by herself. If she continually deviates from socially acceptable behavior, get professional advice.*

INSTILLING RESPONSIBILITY

CHORES

Household chores generally fall into two groups: those that need to be done inside the home and those that need to be done outside. Often a child who is vehemently opposed to doing one type will not mind doing the other.

Everyone who lives in a household should be responsible for its upkeep. Participating in family chores reinforces a sense of responsibility and place in the family. However, don't *ask* your daughter to do something. If you ask and she says "No," you have the beginnings of a confrontation. It is better to *tell* her nicely to do something. "Please take out the garbage" is better than "Do you want to take out the garbage?" You can't expect a "Yes" to that question.

Some children rebel at certain chores. You don't need to teach your daughter that life will beat her down. It is better to teach her

---

*I sometimes recommend seeking professional assistance. That doesn't mean you need to take your daughter to a psychiatrist tomorrow. It does mean that you should immediately discuss the particular situation with your minister, a family doctor, a teacher, school counselor, or a social worker. Get an objective opinion as to your next course of action. They should have lists of organizations and qualified professionals who can help you. Don't be embarrassed. If you feel more comfortable, say you are asking for the information on behalf of someone else—perhaps for your daughter's friend—and want to know the best way to approach the child or her parents.

that she has some control over her life. Most people need to work to earn a living, but that doesn't mean that one's work must be unpleasant. So, if chores need to be done, it doesn't follow that your daughter must do the ones she finds most distasteful. Let her do the ones she finds least objectionable. For example, one of my daughters does not like to do anything that involves stepping out of the apartment once she is home. It would be long faces or semi-scenes if she had to go to the building lobby for the mail or return some milk to a neighbor. She is, however, extremely cooperative about doing dishes or folding laundry. But my other daughter will go out anywhere, anytime (as long as she can wash and blow-dry her hair first).

If there is a particular chore that all members of your household dislike intensely, explain that since everyone hates it, the chore will be shared, or maybe all could take turns doing it. Don't interfere, though, if when your daughter's turn comes she pays one of her sisters or brothers to do the chore for her. Unless the other child, not you, feels an unfair bargain was struck, stay out of the negotiations.

If your daughter procrastinates about doing her chores, try putting a time frame around the job to be done. Instead of badgering her about her promise to clean the gerbil cage, ask her, "What time are you planning to clean the gerbil cage—so I'll know when we can go shopping for your softball uniform." She, therefore, can make the choice of the time she wishes to do the job. The project is under her control. That way you are letting your daughter know you expect her to clean the cage before you take her shopping, but since the decision is hers, she will feel she has some control over her life, not that you boss her around constantly.

Sometimes your daughter will be under extra pressure because of a school play or exams or a special research project. Let the other family members pitch in and take over some of her chores. It's right for her to want to concentrate and do well. Young women have a right to learn that sometimes they deserve special attention. Don't worry about her becoming spoiled. There will be plenty of opportunity for her to take over for you when your life is pressured and hers is not.

HANDLING MONEY

Allowances are marvelous ways for children to learn self-discipline as well as the value of money. An allowance should be given with instructions as to what you expect the money to cover. It should also be of a sufficient amount to allow your daughter to treat a friend to a slice of pizza once in a while. Your daughter should not have to go to you for money on a daily basis, nor should her weekend plans be contingent on your finances at that time. Control by the purse is no control—when the purse is gone, so is the control.

If your daughter does not yet know how to handle money, don't dole it out dollar by dollar. She is not eight years old, and it is time she learned to be responsible for some of her everyday needs and wants. If she is old enough to go to a movie herself, or to a party, she is old enough to budget herself. If she doesn't learn self-discipline about buying hot dogs or makeup, she is going to find it difficult to learn self-discipline with respect to drugs, alcohol and sex. Your daughter must learn how to control her own life. A weekly allowance is a good way to start. Make sure it is given freely and on time. It should not be tied to the doing of chores or given as a reward for certain behavior or grades. Giving an allowance as a ''right'' reinforces your daughter's feeling of self-worth and teaches her how to handle money as well. She should not have to prove her ''worthiness'' each and every time she wants to buy a lipstick or go bowling.

Your daughter's allowance could be expected to cover lunches, carfare, school expenses, entertainment, records, personal items, and gifts for family and friends. Obviously, this adds up to a tidy sum, but the items to be included could be expanded or reduced in accord with your desires and the current level of your daughter's fiscal maturity. Consider also whether her allowance will be supplemented through babysitting or other part-time work.

Your daughter can learn to increase the purchasing power of her allowance by budgeting or planning. For example, when my daughter was in sixth grade, the school allowed her to eat lunch off the premises only one day a week. She eagerly looked forward to junior high, where she would be allowed to eat out every day. All summer she saved her money so she could buy lunch out. However, after spending $10 on lunch the first three days of school, she announced that eating out was a waste of money. She went back to brown bagging it and bought lunch only once a week. She and her friends worked out a system where they would each buy lunch on a different day. The "buyer" was their entree to McDonald's or the local pizzeria; the others opened up their brown bags.

Don't make loans if your daughter overspends during the week and has no money left to go to the movies with her friends on the weekend. That will defeat the purpose of the allowance. You could, however, give her an extra few dollars to spend if her friend is visiting from out of town, or if she has plans to go somewhere with a friend whose family has very little.

Sometimes, though, loans are a good idea. For example, everyone in town has a down vest and your daughter wants one too. You think they are impractical, or you cannot afford it. Let her buy the vest. If she is short on cash, advance her the money and deduct $5 a week until her loan is paid off. Be firm in the deductions. The two of you made a deal and neither of you should welch on it. If she balks at the deduction, remind her that you are not charging interest. Don't waive the balance to be a "good guy." Doing so would void the reasons you initially made the loan.

You could also give a clothing allowance, perhaps three times a year—at the start of school, after Christmas and in May. Discuss your daughter's needs with her and estimate the cost. Add about 20 percent to cover fads or clothing for an unexpected occasion. Be realistic when deciding her needs. Consider local styles, your budget and how easy a fit she is. For example, a slim, flat-chested teen can easily use an inexpensive leotard as a swimsuit, but it might be necessary to spend $50 on a bathing suit if your daughter wears a D cup. Let her do the actual shopping. That way, if she wants six sweaters but only three were budgeted, she has the option of either buying the extra ones with "her" money or learning to buy on sale. (She will also learn to buy wash 'n wear if she does the ironing.)

CURFEWS

Why set curfews? Why do you want your daughter home at a special hour? Are you worried about her getting enough sleep? If so, as an adolescent, that should really be her worry. Are you worried about safety? About sex? Does requiring her to be home at a certain time really guarantee her safety or virginity? I know you don't like to worry. You would love it if your daughter never ventured out at night. A curfew then is really a safety measure, not a test of who's boss.

Your daughter, not you, should be the one to set a curfew. This does not mean she should be allowed to come home any time she wants, but as long as she has a *safe way to return home and the time she sets is reasonable in relation to the activity,* there is no reason to disallow the time she chooses. If, for example, your thirteen-year-old calls and asks if she can see the 10:00 p.m. show because the 8:00 p.m. one is sold out, why not say yes. If she can go to sleep at 1:00 a.m. on school nights and still function, more power to her. If she can't make such a basic decision as to how much sleep she needs, she's going to find it very difficult to make other decisions affecting her well-being.

If she is going to a party and says she will be home at 2:00 a.m. and parties in your community run late, don't make a fuss. If, however, you are a real worrywart and don't think anyone should ever stay out until 2:00 a.m., try a little gentle persuasion. You could point out how much you worry about the safety of the streets at that hour. If you live in a suburban area and don't have the "advantage" of unsafe streets, unsafe drivers will work just as well. Explain that many people who are out late at night probably have had too much to drink and have no business being behind the wheel. Your daughter is no fool, and as long as you assure her it is not her you doubt, but others, she might surprise you and come home a little earlier.

My daughter learned for herself not to stay out too late. She and her friends decided they couldn't go on living unless they saw *The Rocky Horror Picture Show,* which had only a midnight viewing. I offered to meet them (they were all sleeping over at my house), but they wouldn't hear of it. They promised they would take the bus, which stopped in front of the theater and also right in front of our building. They expected to be home no later than 2:30 a.m. Shortly after 3:00 a.m., they came home. I said, "You must have had a long wait for the bus." Silence. Then a squeak. "*Noo,* we stopped for pizza." "At three a.m.!" I exclaimed. Well, it seemed they weren't too thrilled about being out at that hour either. They discovered for themselves that the world can be a pretty scary place at that time. Fortunately, it was a lesson they learned safely.

Many parents don't want their daughters out late because of Sex. I agree. I don't think it is as easy to be sexually active before midnight as after. A sexual relationship is a lot more likely to start after the party's over than before. If the hour your daughter suggests is unreasonable for the activity planned, she may be getting pressure from her boy friend. If she says she will be home at 2:00 a.m. but somehow lets you know the party is to end at 11:00 p.m., she needs you to be the scapegoat. Tell her in no uncertain terms that she is to be home by the hour that you consider reasonable. Give her the excuse she needs. It is much easier for her to tell her boy friend that if she is not home on time she will not be allowed to go out at all than for her to tell him she's not ready for sex yet.

If your daughter refuses to set a curfew and balks if you set one, explain that you need to know when to start worrying. It is your job to make sure she's safe. You are not checking up on her. Don't pretend, though, that a certain time is for her safety when it is for your convenience. If you wait up for your daughter and want her home early, say so. You can simply ask her not to stay out late because you have an early-morning meeting the next day or are worried about something and don't want any additional stress. If you're reasonable in your request, it is likely that she will agree to be home early. She may even surprise you and not go out at all.

You may be the type of person who can't sleep at all when your daughter is out. If so, she will have to learn to live with your limitations. Or you could try a friend's solution. Instead of staying up all night worrying about whether or not her daughter would return safely, she would go to sleep and set her alarm for the time her daughter was expected home. That way, she knew exactly when to start worrying.

BABYSITTING

Babysitting is a good way for your daughter to learn responsibility and to pick up extra money, but it can present problems for you. You must be sure she is ready for the responsibility. You cannot assume that the family she will sit for will tell her everything she needs to know and do. Before your daughter leaves for any sitting job, she should let you know the name and address of the family and when she will come home. Establish a checklist of items that the family is to tell her—emergency phone numbers, names and numbers of doctors, relatives and neighbors, the child's bedtime and bedtime routines, whether any pet needs special care, whether or not friends can visit. Remind your daughter not to tie up the telephone. Warn her not to open the door to strangers or to give out the family name and address to telephone callers, especially to friends who might be interested in mischief. Let your daughter know where you or a friend can be reached in case of an emergency. Besides, it's nice for her to know whom she can call for advice if she has trouble putting the baby to sleep.

You should also tell your daughter not to walk the dog if it means leaving the child alone, not to bathe a five-month-old baby, and not to use the stove if she is sitting for a toddler, even if the parents instructed her to do so. The baby will not develop a rash from missing a bath nor will the toddler develop malnutrition from eating a cheese sandwich for dinner. It's better to clean up after the dog than to risk an accident to the child. Tell your daughter that you don't doubt her capabilities, but there is no reason to take unnecessary risks. Remind her that you too would not leave someone else's child alone to walk a dog, even if the child's parents told you it was fine to do so.

You also need to know how your daughter will get home. This is a major problem today because there are many single parents. While you can check out the people who ask your daughter to sit, you cannot check out the boy friends of the mother who hired her. If your daughter needs to be escorted home, insist that the woman do it. If she can't, go pick her up yourself. This may appear overcautious, but remember, it may be the woman's first date with the man and she may not know him very well either. If your daughter objects to your checking out the people who ask her to sit, or to your picking her up, explain that you don't run the world. Tell her you are not preventing her from sitting. All you are doing is your job—looking out for her safety. If she doesn't want to sit by your rules, remind her she need not take the job.

Other questions arise concerning babysitting, such as whether your daughter should sit on school nights or how late she should be allowed to stay. Unless you are involved in chauffeuring her to and from her jobs, let her set her own schedule and curfew. She needs to learn her own limits. She is not going to want to be too tired to see her friends after school. After two or three late-night jobs which interfere with her life, she will turn down future late ones—and if she can manage to stay out late and get up without being tired, terrific. I wish I could. Remember that she is the one who needs to get up in the morning.

Babysitting can be a big nuisance for you. It can interfere with dinner plans and family activities, but it is worth it. Babysitting will help your daughter to learn to stand up for herself. She will learn to tell parents that she was hired to sit, not to be a maid. She will learn to collect promised money. She will learn to say no to adults who are not honest with her about time. She will also learn how other people live and treat their children.

DRIVING

Whether or not you own a car, your daughter should learn to drive and have the opportunity to drive often. Driving is a necessary skill in our society. Many women who know how to drive cannot drive for long trips, or in the snow, or at night, because of having deferred to their fathers, husbands or boy friends so often. Considering the current divorce rate and the fact that most women will work outside the home at some time during their lives, limited driving skills can seriously interfere with one's career or social life or restrict where one can live.

Using the car should be neither a privilege nor a right. Once your daughter has her license, the family car should be shared in the same way all other family possessions are shared, provided that she is a careful driver. If she isn't, use of the car should be restricted until your daughter understands that being a careful driver means always paying attention and not assuming that the other drivers know how to drive. You cannot expect her to be an expert driver—she does not have enough experience yet. But lack of experience should not prevent her from being careful.

If she is careless when she drives, she should not be permitted to drive. Period. There is no reason for her to endanger her life or the lives of others. Have her take a driver's ed course or have someone drive with her until she learns to appreciate the fact that an automobile is a dangerous weapon.

Don't make the use of the car contingent on her completing her homework or doing certain chores. The homework or chores might get done, but you don't want to take the risk that your daughter would drive too fast to get back at you. You don't want to win the battle of the painted porch and lose the war—in a death or accident resulting from an angrily driven car.

Under no circumstances should you, as a parent, indulge a child who is a careless driver by buying her a car in return for her promises to be careful in the future. She must show that she is not reckless before she can have her own car or use the family car. If she insists on buying her own car, don't put your reckless driver on your insurance policy. She might think twice about being careless when she finds out what the high-risk insurance rates are.

If you and your daughter want the car at the same time, consider letting her drop you off and pick you up instead of the other way around. Maybe she could do some of your chauffeuring and errands. She needs the driving experience and you could always use the extra time.

WORKING

Sooner or later you will nag your daughter about getting a part-time job. Beware of what you will let yourself in for. Most likely, she will find a job the week before your house is to be painted. You may also need to chauffeur her to and fro or rearrange the

67

dinner schedule. You will become her secretary. All her friends will call the minute she comes home, and she will be "too tired" to talk.

Before you tell your daughter about the joys of working, think about it. Do you need her at home? Does her schedule realistically allow it? Will work interfere with her chances for a college scholarship?How much will her work involve you? In many cases it may be necessary for a teen to work. She or her family may really need the money or she may need the self-satisfaction that comes from working. Weigh those things against any upheaval in the family that your daughter's working would cause.

Don't, however, badger your daughter to get a job and be unwilling to help her if she gets one. For example, your fifteen-year-old may find a job in an ice cream parlor and be the one selected to stay after closing time to clean the machines. You will probably need to take her home. Picking her up can turn out to be fun, not a chore. When faced with this situation one couple I know would go out for coffee before picking up their daughter. They said it was like dating again. Also, parents who are alone when they pick up their daughters at a late hour have told me that they and their daughters really talk on the way home. A missed hour of sleep is certainly worth the extra closeness with your spouse or daughter. Of course, if you are a single parent and there are young children at home, it is not reasonable for your daughter to expect you to leave them alone so she can earn some spending money. She will have to find a different job.

Your daughter may be exploited at work. Don't interfere directly. Listen to her and believe her. If she reports that her boss is unfair, it is probably true. Be supportive. Don't tell her it is her fault. Let her work the problem out for herself. It is likely she will not be able to stand up to her boss and will quit instead. Remember, she is only a teenager and exploitation is a new experience for her. Don't expect her to handle it as well as an adult would. Just support her attempts to solve her own problems. You can point out, though, if she quits, that at least she is one of the world's lucky ones. She is sufficiently well off that she can leave a situation where she is exploited. Many people need whatever job they can get—they don't have the luxury of insisting upon being treated fairly.

STAYING ALONE

One day your daughter will insist on staying home alone. In the past, you have been able to convince her to sleep over at a friend's house or have a relative stay with her. This time, though, before you put your foot down and call Great Aunt Mabel or cancel your trip, consider her desires. Your daughter is so anxious to prove to herself and you how grown up she is.

Perhaps she is ready to stay alone. How long will you be away? How safe is your neighborhood? How safe is your home? Will any neighbors be around? How important is it to your daughter? Are younger children involved? For example, I allowed my teen daughters to stay alone for a few days. While they are not friends, there exists a bond of sisterhood between them, so I knew they would look out for each other. Also, my home is relatively safe as we live in an apartment building with a doorman in a nice neighborhood. There are always plenty of neighbors around. However, before I decided, I discussed the situation with a woman who had children the same age as mine and whose opinion I respected. She agreed that she too would leave her daughters alone in similar circumstances, but she would not let them use the stove. I told her in my house the stove was working—it was the toaster whose performance was erratic. (I put the toaster in the closet before I left.)

If you leave your daughter alone, whether it is for a few days or a few hours, make sure she knows what to do in case of an emergency. Leave phone numbers of police, fire, neighbors, doctors and relatives handy. (They should be permanently and prominently listed someplace, anyway.) Leave a number where you can be reached. Make sure she knows never to open the door to strangers or to give out the family name and address to unknown callers. Tell her not to let any callers know she is staying alone. If she will be alone for a day or more, don't arrange for any repairmen to call while you are away. Cancel the gardener. Put away any unsafe appliances. Lock the liquor cabinet. Let her know which friends can visit and whether she may go out and where. Leave extra money.

If you decide your daughter may not stay alone, take care to explain to her that it is not her ability or maturity you doubt (if true), but other circumstances. If these circumstances can be alleviated and you still will not let her stay by herself, your fears may be somewhat irrational. However, you are entitled to be irrational at times. Parenthood does not require you to turn gray so your daughter can prove herself. If, however, you really are holding on too tightly, it may do *you* some good to let go.

VOTING

Many eighteen-year-olds don't bother to vote or even to register. A lot of teens this age are very much "into" themselves and the future is too abstract for them to consider.

Voting is an area where nagging is insufficient. If you remind your daughter that now that she is eighteen she should register to vote, and she responds that she will "When I get around to it," or that "One vote doesn't matter," say no more. *Act* instead. Get the form for her. Even fill it out for her if necessary. Follow her around the house with a pen until she signs it. Mail it for her. If need be, when election day comes, go with her to the polls. If she's away at college, arrange for an absentee ballot. (Many adults need a push to vote, too. On election day the political parties are staffed with volunteers who call registered voters to get out the vote.)

Voting is so important that the goal is not who gets the form or makes the effort, but that the ballot be cast. It is your responsibility to train your daughter to be a responsible citizen. Taking her to the polls with you when she was little was a good start. Take her into the voting booth with you now, so she will realize the process is not as mysterious or intimidating as it may seem. Society cannot afford an apathetic generation. You need to impress upon your daughter that she has a stake in her future and in our complex society. Voting is one way she can be heard.

Also, you might try to get her to participate at the campaign level. Candidates always need volunteers. Even if she works at campaign headquarters only because she has nothing else to do on Friday nights—or because the candidate is cute (or because the other volunteers are)—she may be impressed enough to become committed to the workings of our political process. The charismatic candidate has brought many a young person from complete apathy to political activism. Use issues such as the current cutbacks in student financial aid to galvanize your daughter into political awareness. She may learn that by her own hard work she can help effect change.

HEALTH AND HYGIENE

CLEANLINESS

A short time ago you wondered if your daughter ever really showered. Sure, the curtain was wet, but the soap was dry and the washcloth untouched. Now she is always in the shower—the soap may still be dry, but you know her hair is clean. She also spends an inordinate number of hours in the bathroom washing her face. The medicine cabinet is full of every available acne cream and she has only one pimple so far. However, when you went to borrow a pair of socks from her, you found scads of dirty socks and undies stashed in the dresser drawer. She wears the same jeans every day; brassieres never appear in the wash; but a blouse that needs to be hand-washed and ironed is worn for only two hours before it is tossed into the hamper.

You finally realize that her habits to date have nothing to do with personal cleanliness. To her, cleanliness is still only a question of how she looks, or convenience. Clothes she likes never reach the hamper except just as the washer is to be loaded. (Of course, if she is not home when you do the wash, the favored clothes won't get done until the following week.) She cannot part with a favorite shirt for any longer than the spin cycle. Socks and undies reach the hamper only if it is closer to her than her dresser is when she is getting undressed. It is easier to put a frilly blouse in the hamper than it is to hang it up. She just doesn't think of her body as getting dirty unless she has been rolling in mud.

As she gets older, she discovers that bodies too need to be cleaned. She begins to notice teens who smell or never change their clothes. She becomes loath to share a pizza with a friend whose fingernails are dirty. It dawns on her that showers keep her clean and smelling nice. Now when you enter the bathroom after your daughter has showered, you are overcome by the aromas of lemon shampoo and vanilla bath splash. The air is so thick with talc you can barely breathe. There are little white footprints marking her trail through the house. You now need as many towels as the local Hilton.

Also, sometime during your daughter's adolescence, she will be "sneaky" clean. She will put deodorant on in her closet because you are not supposed to know she uses it. As a matter of fact, she travels with a suitcase between her room and the bathroom. She is not to be seen even carrying a bra, let alone wearing one. She is so shy about her person she doesn't even admit to liking a special shampoo. (Don't worry—once she gets over this phase, her brand of deodorant and shampoo will appear on *your* shopping list.) She is so shy that she has a real problem in disposing of used sanitary napkins, especially at school. Be sensitive to her. Today, the restrooms in many junior and senior high-schools cannot be used. Ignore her stained clothes. She knows she needs to change her pads more often, but it may not be possible for her to do so. Be tactful when she expresses embarrassment about carrying extra pads with her. After all, she might get run over and someone will go through her book bag and *know*.

As your daughter gets more comfortable with her physical development, her shyness and self-consciousness will disappear. If, however, she should be using a deodorant and isn't, or is still wearing knee socks to the beach to cover her hairy legs, buy her the appropriate aids and leave them on her dresser or in her closet. Buy a well-known nondescript brand, not the "special for the teen" variety. What she wants now is not to be singled out. If you notice that she has used the items you bought for her, make no comment. If she hasn't, try again in a month or so. If then she still won't use a deodorant, tell her she must . . . and that you are sorry to step on her feelings. Tell her she is going to grow up whether she wants to or not. Remind her there are some advantages to being an adult—you're more your own boss, no homework, you don't have to worry about exams or growing up, you get to meet a lot of interesting people, you can have children, see whatever movie you want—it is not all paying taxes and worrying.

BAD HABITS

Your daughter may have a bad habit such as biting her fingernails or twirling her hair. Nag, threaten, rant and rave as you will, but the nail biting and hair twirling will continue. Bribery may work temporarily, but not as a long-term solution.

The solution must be totally up to your daughter because it is *her* problem. She could plan to buy herself a present if she stops biting her nails for a month. If she works hard and breaks her habit she deserves to "treat" herself.

Encourage her to set a goal with a specific reward in mind. Perhaps she would like a 35 mm camera but has been hesitant to buy one because it seems so extravagant. Leave everything in her control so that if she cures herself of nail biting, she will have every reason to feel terrific about herself. She need not share her accomplishment with anyone else. Every time she uses the camera she will feel proud of herself. The camera and her nice nails will always be a reminder that she had a problem that she alone solved. If she tries to stop but doesn't succeed, nothing has been lost. Just suggest that she try again a few months later.

EXERCISE

If I had it to do over again, I would have incorporated exercise into my children's daily personal routine, just as I did teeth brushing and bed making. Unfortunately I didn't, and my teen daughter considers it exercise to hand-wind a clock. Suggestions about jogging, tennis, cycling, daily calisthenics or walking go unheeded. My daughter contends that she gets plenty of exercise walking up and down the stairs at school. However, the only activity that I'm aware of is her mouth moving.

I do know several teen girls who are active. They are the girls who excel at a particular sport or physical activity. Many girls, though, are self-conscious and inhibited when it comes to using their body. A young girl's insecurity often prevents her from doing anything that she may not do well. Don't rush to blame your daughter's self-consciousness on your failing as a ''modern parent,'' just because you may not be as open about sex or feminine hygiene as you think you should be. Remember, your daughter may have developed earlier than her friends, or may experience hoots and whistles way before she is emotionally ready for them. She may be walking around looking for lost kittens to rescue, with thoughts of boys still a few years away, but that doesn't prevent her from being whistled at.

It *is* a shame that so many beautiful young bodies will turn to flab much sooner than they need to. Teens, however, are short-sighted and they see themselves lean and firm now and forever. Cajoling your daughter into swimming or exercise class may turn out to be a waste of money even if she has some interest in the activity. I know a young girl who cuts her belly-dancing class. You'd think no one would take belly-dancing unless they wanted to, but she doesn't just quit because she doesn't want to listen to her mother nag her about being a bump on a log.

Until your daughter finds out her mistake for herself, the best you can do is keep nagging, go easy on the calories and hope for the best. Maybe someday she will surprise you and suggest that the two of you enroll in an aerobics class. You'd better be ready!

PHYSICAL DEVELOPMENT

The growth of the human body is very capricious during the adolescent years. The changes occurring in your daughter's body will affect her behavior. They will make her feel unattractive and self-conscious. She will feel she is too tall, too skinny, too short, too fat, too flat-chested, too busty.

Breast development particularly will impact on an adolescent's social behavior more than any other physical change. If your daughter develops early, she may be cast off by her childhood friends. Her early development will scare them and they will find her freakish. She will become overly self-conscious and critical. Sweaters and T-shirts will reveal too much of what she would like to hide. Bathing suits are definitely not made for her body. She

74

will feel she will forever be left out by the "in" crowd, the beautiful people. She will look at today's media blitz and see only the Brooke Shieldses of the world and the slim jeaneration.

Your words to the effect that everyone has their own development schedule and that soon her friends will catch up will offer her little consolation. Be patient and understanding. She will even be embarrassed to shop for a bra. Allow your daughter her modesty and do the bra purchasing for her. Don't tease her or tell her she will be the next Raquel Welch. Remember, she may have an adult body, but she is still a child. Forcing her to accept her sexuality before she is emotionally ready might cause her to be sexually active far too soon.

If your daughter is a late developer physically, it may follow that her social development and interest in boys lag behind her peers. Along with all her other adolescent worries and problems, she may no longer have Nancy, who was her best friend from first to eighth grade, to rely on. Your daughter may feel totally left out and not want to make friends with those whose development is similar to hers because they may often be a year or two younger than she. She looks at the world around her and sees only the Playboy bunnies and sexy underwire bras.

As with the early developer, your words about individual development schedules will offer little, if any, consolation. Be tactful. Don't criticize her for not keeping her old friends or encourage her to make friends with those a grade or two behind her. Instead, help her to expand her interests. Soon she will meet others who are the same age as she and at a similar stage physically. Point out that she too could have boy friends if she wanted. There are plenty of fifteen-year-old boys around who have not begun to grow tall; boys who still are more interested in hitting a baseball than talking to a girl. Your daughter's lack of sexuality will make them feel very comfortable. For example, I know a fourteen-year-old physically immature girl who was going on a bike tour with a coed group of fourteen- to seventeen-year-olds. Some of the girls were real knockouts and a few of the boys were already six-footers. My young friend approached the group timidly. She was, however, eagerly greeted by two boys no taller than she. The three of them all breathed deep sighs of relief.

MENSTRUATION

Some girls have no problem adjusting to becoming a woman. Some girls welcome it and eagerly look forward to wearing their first bra. However, some girls regard menstruation as a personal affront and feel resentful about being female. If your daughter has these latter feelings, it will do no good to tell her about the wonders of love and motherhood. It is too far away. Right now she is embarrassed and confused. Protruding breasts and hair on her legs make her self-conscious. She probably refuses to wear a bra, or if she does, she doesn't want anyone to know. Treat her gently and don't buy a white dimity blouse for her to wear. Army shirts and knee socks are *de rigueur*.

She also probably envies her male friends because they don't have her "problem." They don't have to worry about anyone "seeing anything" through their clothes. If your daughter feels this way, explain to her that boys also go through embarrassment during their adolescence. She probably knows a fourteen-year-old boy who looks ten and another who looks like a full-grown man. Tell her about the boys' locker room games and ask her how she thinks the small fourteen-year-old feels in a "how high can you squirt" contest. Explain a boy's changing feelings toward females and mention how self-conscious he must be about someone noticing his erection when a girl passes close to him, or even worse, when a female teacher passes by.

Once your daughter understands that puberty happens to boys as well as girls, she will not feel singled out. Even if she still regards menstruation as a "gross" nuisance, she will not feel so negative about being female. She still, however, may feel embarrassed about buying her own supplies for menstruation. Make sure there is a supply of whatever she uses in the house. Little by little she will feel more comfortable with her femaleness. She may start mentioning the "unmentionable" by asking you to buy a particular brand of pad. Later, she may tell you she can't go to the pool because she "has her period" rather than "*you know.* . . ." She may ask your advice about using tampons.* For

* Because of the recent occurrences of toxic-shock syndrome, check with your doctor about the advisability of tampon use.

example, my fourteen-year-old wanted to know how to insert a tampon because she was going to be in Florida while she had her period and she wanted to be able to go swimming. However, her muscles contracted and she wasn't able to. I told her not to worry, her body simply wasn't ready—she could try again when she was older. The slender style is in the closet when she's ready to try again.

If you maintain a matter-of-fact attitude about menstruation, after your daughter recovers from the newness of it, she too will treat it without any undue concern.

PSYCHIATRY AND PSYCHOLOGY

This book covers fairly typical female adolescent behavior. It does not discuss in any depth why adolescent girls behave the way they do, nor is the book meant to be a substitute for psychological counseling if there is an indication that your daughter is in need of it.

Probably everyone could benefit from some psychological counseling or some form of therapy, but don't *threaten* your daughter that she needs a psychiatrist. If you believe she has problems that she is unable to handle even with your help, don't hesitate to get professional help. Simply explain to your daughter that it is not a punishment or a disgrace to visit a psychiatrist. Say that as a parent it is your job to help her. Your arranging for her to visit a psychiatrist or psychologist, for example, is no different from your taking her to a doctor for a broken leg or paying for her allergy injections. If, however, you remind her that no one else in the family needs counseling or make her feel guilty about the expense, she may refuse to go. If you have a positive attitude, she is more likely to have one also, and will, therefore, be able to receive the maximum benefit from the counseling.

A friend's twelve-year-old daughter was having trouble dealing with her parents' divorce and the subsequent sale of the family house and move to another city. The girl became extremely difficult to manage. She was also verbally abusive to her mother and took to twirling her hair to the point that a bald spot developed.

Perhaps the parents could have managed their break-up better. Perhaps the girl was using the divorce as an excuse for her behavior. Neither is the issue. The girl needed help. Wisely, the parents, instead of each trying to blame the other for her behavior or insisting that she handle the problem herself, sought psychiatric help.

The parents' positive behavior concerning their daughter's problem gave her the support she needed to be able to benefit from the doctor's guidance.

NUTRITION

Nutrition is an area where actions speak louder than words. Potato chips, hot dogs, cake and candy bars have no business being in anyone's home today on a regular basis. If you buy boxes of cookies, don't expect them to be eaten one cookie at a time. Teens eat compulsively, just as they do everything else. Don't keep non-nutritious food stocked in the pantry. Such foods can be bought sparingly as the occasion calls for them. If your daughter loves to snack, keep a plate of fresh vegetables and dip prepared in the refrigerator. Stock the refrigerator with low-fat yoghurt, fresh fruit, roasted chicken wings or drumsticks. Your daughter will be ravenous after school and will grab the easiest thing to eat. She may as well eat nourishing food instead of junk.

You can also satisfy your daughter's sweet tooth nutritionally. Bananas and applesauce cake are delicious. Also good are home-made whole wheat and fruit muffins or peanut butter or oatmeal cookies. Raisins and nuts can be added for extra nutrition. You can do your baking with half the sugar and unbleached flour. Wheat germ can be substituted for the missing sugar.

Shop carefully and make sure the fruit and vegetables you buy are fresh. If that's not possible, the frozen kind are almost as good. You can help keep calories to a minimum. For example, when serving potatoes, serve them baked or boiled with the skin. They can be seasoned with low-fat sour cream or margarine instead of butter. Nutritionists advise eating fish and poultry instead of red meat. If the only poultry your daughter will eat is chicken, that's okay; ditto if tuna is the only fish she will eat. She doesn't need to eat squab or sardines. Avoid arguments and don't try to be too adventurous with your daily meal planning. Some adolescents have very limited food preferences. Sometimes their tastes are strange—they may range from the basic peanut butter and jelly sandwiches to steak tartare or raw fish. Or your daughter may completely change her eating habits from one day to the next. Since early childhood she may have eaten very little else besides hamburgers, hot dogs and bologna sandwiches, but may one day decide to become a vegetarian. Another teen whose taste buds never ventured beyond American cheese or mashed potatoes may agree to go with you to the new Chinese restaurant. Don't be surprised, however, if her idea of gourmet Chinese food is wonton soup and a bowl of white rice. Be patient and keep in mind that today's adult gourmet probably started out ordering chow mein as an adolescent.

If your daughter complains that "there is nothing to eat in this house" (translation: no pretzels, soda, salami, ice cream or cookies), let her do the shopping. Give her what you would normally spend for the week's groceries and challenge her to do better. Explain that she needs to choose so that the family will be well nourished—but she can buy what she wants with any money that is left over. You'll find that, given the responsibility, your daughter will rise to the occasion and surprise you. She may even do a better job than you.

What and when we eat plays a very important part in our culture. It's only natural to want to bring home a triple chocolate cake to celebrate a raise. However, when you are tempted to do something like that, tell yourself that loving your family does not mean bringing home something that is not good for them. Satisfy those urges by bringing home fruit or nuts. For example, honeydew melons and raspberries have been beyond my budget for a long time. When I bring them home, it's appreciated as much as any jelly donuts. Sometimes I buy exotic or gourmet food when I'm in the mood to bring home a treat—perhaps a papaya or an unusual cheese. Sometimes we don't like the exotica and it gets thrown out, but the thought was there and we enjoyed ourselves as much as if we had double-dipped into peppermint ice cream (well, almost as much).

PARTY FOOD AND DRINK

Party food can be as nutritious as regular food. Teens just like to keep their mouths going and are not particularly choosy as long as the food is not "fancy" or "too mushy."

Fresh cut vegetables served with a tangy yoghurt dip are a good substitute for potato chips and packaged dips. Mushrooms stuffed with cheese or sautéed onions make a nice hot hors d'oeuvre. Bowls of popcorn are good to have scattered around, as are bowls of raisins mixed with dry-roasted nuts, and trays of fresh fruit with crackers and cheese. Pizza or pasta makes a nutritious main dish. Also popular as main party dishes are baked potatoes served with stuffings such as sour cream, Cheddar cheese or chili, or yoghurt served with a variety of toppings such as raisins, nuts, fruits and wheat germ or granola. Drinks can consist of juices such as apple, orange, grapefruit or cranberry, served plain or with club soda. Milk is always popular with boys if it's in view. You could also serve white grape juice on the rocks or mineral water with a twist of lemon for a more sophisticated atmosphere.

If your daughter is adamant about serving junk food, serve *some*. Just keep it to a minimum and don't refill the bowls and trays when the first servings are gone. Instead, serve popcorn, fruits and nuts or cheese and crackers as replacements.

If your daughter says she won't have the party unless beer is served, don't have the party. You cannot serve alcohol to minors. It is also your responsibility to see that the teens do not go out to the cars to guzzle up. Be careful to check the outside activity and confiscate any alcohol. If you find someone drinking who is supposed to drive home, drive that teen home or call the parents to come pick him or her up. Alcohol and driving do not mix. Explain to any who might be embarrassed by you (your daughter) or take offense at your actions (the drinker) that you care enough about all of them to risk their displeasure. Let them know that attending a funeral the next day is not your idea of a fun way to spend your time.

WEIGHT

Teen girls are never satisfied with what they weigh. They feel they are either too thin or too fat. Your daughter may very well *be* too thin or too fat. If so, the first thing you should do is take her for a medical checkup. Most likely there is no physical reason for your daughter's weight problem and the doctor will prescribe an appropriate diet and exercise regimen. However, it is up to your daughter to follow the doctor's advice. Her weight is her problem, not yours. Don't badger your daughter to gain or lose weight. Improper weight is often caused by psychological problems—even minor ones. Don't add to your daughter's discomfort by causing unnecessary friction between the two of you.

Your daughter can learn to control her weight by modifying her eating habits, without conquering all the causes of her under- or overeating. You can help her to change her eating habits. Teach your daughter to eat properly. Make sure the home environment will assist her in solving her problem. For example, if she is too thin because she doesn't eat enough, make sure the mealtime atmosphere is pleasant. Keep her at the table as long as possible. Don't pick on her for not eating or for poor table manners. You will destroy the atmosphere you have tried to create. Serve meals family-style and encourage second helpings. The food need not be fattening or special, just attractively served.

If your daughter is overweight, you should still try to make mealtime as pleasant as possible, but don't encourage lingering after the meal is finished. Serve meals restaurant-style so she is not tempted to take a second helping. If she does, though, don't make a scene. You don't want to give her an excuse to leave the table and "finish her dinner" later—when, instead of another chicken wing, she fixes herself a liverwurst sandwich.

The food you serve need not be diet food. The rest of the family needs to eat too. Just make sure the meals you plan are nutritious and do not contain unnecessary calories. There is no need to serve broccoli with a rich cheese sauce along with a meat dish—a sprinkling of grated cheese will do just as well. If the rest of the family can handle desserts without gaining weight, by all means serve them. However, make sure that there are no left-overs. Don't tempt your daughter by keeping wedges of cheese-cake in the refrigerator. You might even want to suggest that she leave the table while everyone else is eating dessert.

If she is on a special diet, your daughter should still eat her meals with the rest of the family. Try to see that her diet meal contains as many courses as the family meal. Take special care to make her cottage cheese and lettuce look attractive. A sprig of mint or parsley will help. You want her to feel satisfied emotion-ally, as well as physically, after she has eaten.

Don't keep a bare refrigerator because your daughter needs to lose weight. The refrigerator should be well stocked with healthy and easy-to-prepare snacks as suggested under Nutrition (page 78). She needs to lose weight now, but more important, she needs to learn to control her appetite.

What she also needs is your support and encouragement. If she wants to keep you apprised of her day-to-day losses, listen, but don't comment except with a smile or a "That's nice, dear." If she has setbacks, don't make her feel guilty. Support her by saying that tomorrow is another day and by telling her how well she has done so far. Remind her about the meals she ate properly and the snacks she skipped. Tell her not to allow a day or two of binging to destroy all her hard work. If she wants to put signs on the refrigerator or a full-size picture of herself in a bathing suit on the living room wall, let her.

If your daughter just talks about dieting but never does, don't make her feel guilty for not following through. You will only add to her lack of self-esteem. Remember, her poor eating habits and improper attitude about food were a long time in the making. It will be very difficult for her to change her ways. You do your part by being reasonable with respect to food, and by being consider-ate and thoughtful in how you treat her; sooner or later she will take the initiative herself. Of course, there's nothing wrong with the gentle art of persuasion as long as you are not "so subtle" that you are cruel. It would be wrong for you to buy her a suede pants outfit two sizes too small for her. If she wants to buy it for herself as an incentive, that's fine. If you bought the outfit, you would be putting her weight in your control and it isn't—it's in her control. There is, however, nothing wrong with suggesting (not forcing) that she spend her summer at a weight-control camp. She has to do something for the summer, and sticking to the camp's regimen would be her responsibility, not yours. Your only responsibility would be to pay for it.

5
IT'S HER LIFE, BUT...

SCHOOL

HOMEWORK

Too many parents feel their daughter's homework is *their* responsibility. It isn't. It's your daughter's. Your responsibility ends with providing time (and space if possible) for her to do it. Also, if you want to, and are permitted to, you can be a sounding board for her essays and speeches. You can even help type reports if, for example, time pressures are such that she winds up with two papers to do on the same weekend.

It is understandable that you want your daughter to study and do well. However, she's the one taking the exams and, therefore, the one who must do the work. It's also true that some teens need more nagging than others. I'm not against nagging. It shows concern, and your motives are honorable. What is wrong, though, is treating your teenager like a baby with such threats as, "If you don't get a B in English, you can't go to the dance." Better to say, "If you don't get a B, your choice of college or jobs will be limited . . . it's your life." She needs to begin to learn that how she behaves as a teen will impact on her whole life, not just the following Saturday night. You need to help her realize that there is such a thing as life after high school.

There's nothing wrong with a little bribery, but be realistic. It should be given for a job well done. For example, I paid my daughter, who was a mediocre student, $5 for every final B, $10 for a final A and $15 for a B average. I knew she would have to work hard to earn the money. She asked me if I would pay her $25 for an A average. I told her no . . . I would give her $100! We had a good chuckle and I was happy to know she could view her own limitations with humor. Also, just because you give one child monetary encouragement doesn't mean you need to do the same for your other children. You should treat your children as individuals. My other daughter, an honor student, wanted to know why I didn't pay her for good grades. I responded that her "reward" was never needing to worry that she had failed an exam.

You might want to monitor the time your daughter spends on homework. If she never seems to have any, or has very little, and there is no indication that she is not doing her assignments, you should consider pressuring the school to assign more work. Your daughter should not receive make-work homework, but you and she have a right to expect her school lectures to be reinforced. She is obligated by law to go to school until a certain age. You and your community should be diligent in your efforts to ensure that the school fulfills its obligation to her. Constructive homework can clarify learning. Your daughter will also learn to be responsible about handing in assignments and budgeting her time. And, if she is one of those children who do not know how to use free time to their advantage, time spent on homework will be less spent on the telephone or in front of the television, or will give her less time to get into trouble.

GRADES

Your daughter's grades are as much a reflection of whether she has accommodated the teacher as of what she has learned. However, consider any grade under a C as an indication that the teacher is not effectively communicating the subject matter to her.

If your daughter receives less than a C and complains that the teacher marks her down because she doesn't like her, or because she doesn't hand in her homework, tell her only A students can afford those luxuries. If your daughter's grades don't pick up by the next marking period, get a tutor. She should be learning enough about a subject to warrant at least a C, no matter whether the subject matter is exceedingly difficult or the teaching exceedingly poor.

However, if you think your daughter is smart but her grades are mediocre, be objective. Is she really underachieving or are your expectations too high? Remember, she may have a lot of common sense and native intelligence and understanding of human nature, but that does not translate into scholastic A's. Don't tell your C or B student that she's not working hard enough. True, a little more work may earn her a C + or a B + occasionally, but hard work usually does not transform a C student into an A student. Teens who have the capability to get A's usually do so.

You may need to do a little pushing and shoving if you and your daughter got into the push-and-shove game during her elementary-school years and you feel it's not worth the effort to break past patterns. Besides, some children do need more prodding than others. If you find you do need to push and shove, or your daughter likes you to, fine. Just keep it in perspective. Don't tell her she didn't study hard enough when she gets a D on her final after doing B work all semester. She may not be capable of reviewing and retaining an entire semester's work in time for the final exam.

Unless your daughter is planning to attend a competitive university, focus more on what she is learning than on what grade she is receiving. Allow her the right not to hand in her homework and take a B instead of an A if she feels like it. If, however, your daughter is planning on attending a competitive institution, she cannot afford the luxury of standing on principle and not doing make-work homework if her grades will suffer as a result. True, she may be fortunate enough to receive A's with a minimum of effort, no matter how difficult the course, but is frustrated about not being challenged. Empathize with her about doing make-work. Explain that it may not be make-work for the other students but agree that it is unfair for her teacher to mark her down for not doing work she does not need to do. (It is too bad that these teens are not challenged more instead. If you have the time, try to get the school to pay more attention to the bright students.)

Be aware of a sharp drop in grades; your daughter may be having social problems at school or be involved with drugs or alcohol. However, don't treat every slump in performance as a major catastrophe or as a signal that something awful is going on. She may just feel overworked or bored or both and want a few weeks off. If she is open enough to let you know how boring school is or what a waste of time she thinks it is, she is probably taking a needed break from routine. It's doubtful she has anything to hide. All you need to do is listen—but if her slump continues for more than one marking period, check her overall health. She shouldn't be *that* bored.

DROPPING OUT

All along your daughter has been a model student. She always got straight A's and approached her school and social life eagerly. However, at some time during school (most likely when she is a high-school junior or a college sophomore), she will think seriously about chucking it all. What she is learning seems pointless. Her life has no meaning. You could call it the "Why am I here?" syndrome.

Take your daughter's feelings seriously. Don't think that because she does well in school, she will have the sense to be future-oriented. Her feelings may seem simplistic and superficial to you, but they are very real to her. You can help her by pointing out that everyone feels that way at one time or another—even as an adult. Tell her about the time you planned on abdicating your role as mother. You even went as far as buying the bus ticket. Explain that what kept you from leaving was understanding that your feelings, though very intense and real, were temporary. Encourage her to stick it out. Tell her you don't have the answers for her, but in time she will have them for herself. All she needs to do is hang in there a little longer.

While she's a potential dropout, try not to be too cheerful. That will only make her feel her melancholy even more. Treat her as if she were recovering from a not too serious virus—with patience, firmness and kindness, but without being solicitous.

87

Keep reiterating that she won't feel the way she does forever.

If your daughter wants to drop out of high school because of poor grades or social problems, encourage her to attack the problem rather than walk away from it. Perhaps she will agree to tutoring. Consider also that her poor grades may reflect problems in her home or social life. Professional assistance might be advisable. Or, she may want to drop out because it seems glamorous to work or because she needs more pocket money. If so, help her get a part-time job. You might need to release her from some of her chores, or pick her up at late hours from a job, but it's worth it to keep her in high school.

If your daughter arrives home from college and doesn't want to return because of the "What does it all mean?" syndrome, encourage her to return, but don't turn the situation into a major confrontation. If you handle her despondency with tact and understanding and do not turn it into a battle, it is likely she can be persuaded to return to college (perhaps a local one) by the start of the following semester. Also, if you are tactful and understanding you will be able to convince her to resume her studies even if her proposed exodus from college was prompted by poor grades. Encourage her to try again, perhaps in an easier program or with the assistance of a tutor. Don't let her feel like a failure. Failing a semester may be expensive, but it is not tantamount to failing at life. A college education is so important today that even if all you convince her to do is to continue her studies part-time while she works, you will have succeeded. Explain that the real advantage of a college degree, even if she doesn't want to be "anything" now, is that it will give her the option to be "something" when she's older. At the least, a college degree will offer her a choice.

If your daughter feels finishing high school and then going to college may be too much school to endure just so she can have a choice when she's older, do what a friend of mine did. She prevented her sixteen-year-old daughter from dropping out by taking her to the law firm where she worked as a secretary. She showed her daughter her boss's impressive office—couch, coffee table, big oak desk, thick carpet—and said, "This is where you sit if you finish graduate school." Next, she took her daughter to a paralegal's office, which was simply and efficiently furnished with a desk, wall unit and two easy chairs, and stated,

"This is where you sit if you finish college." Next, she took her to her "station" which was equipped with a standard secretarial desk, typewriter and armless chair, and said, "This is where you sit if you finish high school." Next and last, they visited the mail room. There was no carpet, no private telephone, no chairs— only noisy machines, musty odors, lots of dust and a few ugly stools. She told her daughter, "This is where you sit if you drop out of high school." Needless to say, the visit was very effective.

Her *Goldilocks and the Three Bears* solution may seem crass and simplistic, nor is graduate school or college the only route to success. However, the mother's immediate problem was to impress upon her daughter the need to stay in high school, and "a picture is worth a thousand words."

CHOOSING A CAMP

Your daughter is a teen and has never been to camp and decides she wants to go, or she has gone before but now wants to go to a different camp. It is best for her not to break into a "traditional" camp at this age. Cliques will have been formed and she will feel out of place. Look for camps that have specific programs beginning with the teen years. Also, the camp should group campers by interest or school grade rather than by chronological age. This can prevent a lot of heartache if your thirteen-year-old daughter will be a tenth grader but was grouped with thirteen-year-old ninth graders, or if her best friend who is in her grade is going to the same camp but is placed in an older group because she is six months older than your daughter.

Don't pick out a camp that *you* would like. Your role is to find out the types of camps available which are in your price range and meet your standards with respect to health facilities and association certification or licensing. Let your daughter select the camp from those which you find acceptable. After all, she is the one who will be going. Besides, if the camp turns out to be a dud, she cannot blame you. Also, if it was her selection, she is more likely to accept less than expected—it's important not to lose face.

My daughter and her friend selected a wilderness camp for their first camp experience. I was amazed because their only contact with nature until then had been picking fruit from the supermarket bins. I thought the idea was terrific, but I had plenty of doubts as to whether my daughter would like it. I decided not to intervene. The camp was accredited and had a good reputation. I did not feel it was my parental duty to describe outhouses and cold showers or "separation stops" (peeing in the woods). Neither did I feel it my responsibility to describe how uncomfortable it is to sleep on the floor of a cave without the benefit of a cot nor how uncomfortable it could be carrying a full pack and fighting off mosquitoes in 95° weather. At best, all such comments would do would be to dissuade her from going and she would lose an opportunity to find out about herself. She did seem a little hesitant though, when as she was leaving, I slipped a roll of toilet paper into her backpack.

My silence was wise. She loved the suffering. She was so proud of herself. She even wanted to return the following summer. She learned how to canoe, how to survive in the woods, how to get along with people she didn't like, how to handle fear and discomfort. I learned that it is as wrong to impose my own doubts about my daughter's abilities on her as it would be to impose my own expectations on her.

CHOOSING A COLLEGE

Picking and choosing and being accepted into a college may be a bigger trauma for girls in the Northeast than in other parts of the country simply because of the proximity of many Ivy and Little Ivy League colleges. In any event, the thought of going off to college is traumatic. Soon after the excitement of selecting the colleges and mailing the applications wears off, your daughter is in for a shock. All along she has been looking forward to going away, but now it dawns on her that going away to school means she won't be living at home any more . . . *and she's scared*. She realizes that soon she really will be grown-up and have to take care of herself. Reassure her that it is normal for her to feel apprehensive and that her home will always be her home no matter where she lives. Don't tell her you plan to convert her room to a guest room or redecorate it to her sister's taste. (Such things shouldn't be done until it is clear that your daughter considers college her home—maybe when she is a junior or senior. In the meantime, she should know that she has a home base to return to.)

If your daughter plans to go away to school and has never been away from home, insist that she go away for at least part of the summer between her junior and senior high-school years. Perhaps she can be a camp counselor or a mother's helper. Many colleges have special summer programs for high-school students. Most teens will enjoy the experience of being away. Some, however, are very upset by it. It is better for them to be miserable for four weeks than for four months. Going away to college is not for everyone. Your daughter should not feel like a failure if she wants to attend a local institution. If she does attend college while living at home, though, give her as much freedom as possible and protect her as little as possible. She will need to leave sometime, and it's part of your job to prepare her to leave the nest. Some girls just need more preparation than others.

You and your daughter should be realistic when choosing a college. You both may want Princeton, but so do thousands of others. Realize that the competition for some schools is extremely tough and while your daughter may have all the qualifications, she still may not be selected. If she isn't accepted by a highly competitive institution, don't drown her with *your* disappointment. Don't remind her that you told her to wear something different for the interview, or that she shouldn't have babysat the night before she took her SATs. She feels bad enough.

Generally, do not interfere with the choice of colleges your daughter selects to apply to unless they are unacceptable because of distance or expense, or have a valid reputation as a drug haven or for having wild parties. Also, don't let your daughter select schools whose standards are obviously too low for her capability and scholastic performance.

If your daughter is planning to go to a private college or a highly competitive public university, it is likely that you are going to be much more involved in the application process than you anticipated. Some high-school college counseling services are woefully inadequate. They may actually discourage applications to private colleges because of the paperwork involved. If your daughter knows where she wants to apply, fine. If not, your local library should have a college index by majors. You can buy college guide books which give brief descriptions of U.S. and Canadian colleges—size, admission standards, location, courses offered, costs, student life, etc. Once a group of schools are selected, follow up to see that your daughter and her school mail in their respective application sections on time. (Many colleges send acknowledgment of an application soon after its receipt.) Some girls delay mailing the application to their first-choice school because of fear of being rejected. If your daughter is dillydallying, explain this as a possible reason and encourage her to mail it in anyway. After all, if the application never gets mailed, she certainly will never attend that school.

If your daughter has the minimum requirements for her first-choice college, a preapplication call to that school's admission office might help. Would she have a better chance of getting accepted if she applied for General Studies instead of Business? Would a personal interview help? Perhaps a letter explaining that her poor junior-year grades were due to illness (if true) or reference letters from her employers or from associations for which she did volunteer work would help. Also, a letter from your daughter saying it's her first-choice college might move her application from the "maybe" stack to the "yes" stack.

If despite everyone's efforts your daughter is not accepted by a school she really wants to attend, suggest she write a letter expressing her disappointment and request that her application be reconsidered—but only if there are extenuating circumstances which would warrant a reconsideration. For example, your daughter's poor grades or lack of extracurricular activities might have been the result of the death of a parent, your recent divorce, drug rehabilitation, or her frequent change of schools. She has nothing to lose by asking for a reconsideration, but if she is reluctant to do so, don't push her.

You must be very patient while your daughter is waiting for her acceptance letters. This is a very tense time for her, as she will take any rejection as a rejection of *her,* not merely of her application. Because so many teens feel that a college rejection letter is a personal rejection, you may not want your daughter to interview at a school where her qualifications are borderline. If her application is later rejected, it will be twice as hard for her not to feel it personally.

Your daughter may not be college material. However, if she's a C student and wants to go to college, don't discourage her. College is never a waste of time. She will at least learn more about herself and something about others and the world. However, if your daughter is a C student and has no desire to go to college, don't force her to. Remind her, though, that if you live in a metropolitan area, a college degree (even a two-year degree), is a must for almost any job paying more than the minimum wage. If your daughter is reluctant to attend college, bring home some brochures from the community colleges. Courses offered at these schools are of a more practical nature and she might find something that interests her. Explain that if she is so eager to work, she may as well do something she enjoys. Suggest she work and take one course at the school. Make sure she starts out with a course that is different from what she studied in high school. English Composition might be a poor choice, but Introduction to Real Estate may not be. She may surprise herself and really enjoy school for the first time.

FREE TIME

TOO LITTLE. During the school year your daughter is involved in many after-school activities. She's on the swim team and she tutors Spanish. She works for her uncle on Saturdays and she's active in your church's youth group. Now she tells you she tried out for a supporting role in the school play. She has no time to think or to dream or to spend with you. You feel she's like a stretched-out rubber band—ready to snap at any moment.

You can help her by setting aside some time for her to do nothing. For example, no one in our house makes plans for Sunday evenings. We use it as a time to get ready for the week. It's the time to do hand wash, try purple nail polish or thumb through old magazines. Sometimes we play double solitaire. It's a good time too to discuss the upcoming week, so other family members will know if any extra demands are to be made on their time. Try to arrange a similar time in your home when the whole family can be together doing nothing, so the stress of the following week can be reduced as much as possible.

TOO MUCH. Your daughter announces she's not going to camp this summer—she's going to get a job. Terrific. But what if she does not get a job? You cannot let her just "hang out" for three months. Her days must have some structure. Insist on an alternative—riding lessons, courses, a different camp, visits to friends or relatives—but make it clear that she cannot just do nothing all summer.

She need not have all her time filled, nor need it be filled unpleasantly. For example, she can take a lifesaving course and babysit a few afternoons a week. Just make sure there is some focus to most of her days.

If your daughter is reluctant to make a commitment to a particular summer activity, arrange or suggest volunteer work. Generally, teens are selfish with respect to their efforts and your daughter will probably balk at doing something for nothing. Tell her the choice is hers: either she finds something to do that interests her or she does volunteer work. Explain that it is your job to see that her body and mind function twelve months a year, not just nine.

READING

For your daughter, reading may have become a lost art. Television and movies take her places where only books took us before. However, books foster the use of imagination in a way that movies and television cannot. It's important that your daughter read *something*, even if it is only a fashion magazine or a television listing. Explain to her that reading is valuable even today because it fires the imagination and develops vocabulary. Also, knowledge learned from reading, no matter how trivial, makes even a boring person interesting. For example, if she reads a sports magazine or the sports pages in the local newspaper, her boy friend will probably think she is the most interesting female he has ever met.

If your daughter is not a reader, it may be because she associates reading with learning and doesn't equate learning with pleasure. You can help her develop the habit of reading by bringing home the newspaper every day and asking her to look through it for store coupons or the weather report. While browsing through the paper for you, she may find articles that interest her. Buy a variety of magazines and best-sellers and leave them lying around after you've read them. Ask her to find articles for you— perhaps on decorating if you are thinking of some changes in house decor. Read some of the books that her group might be interested in and describe them to her. If she is given a reading list for the summer to be completed by the time school starts, show an interest in her choices and help her locate the books if the local library or paperback book stores don't have them.

When she does read, don't criticize her for reading things that are too easy for her, or for not getting from her reading what others do in terms of the "message." For example, my daughter chose *The Diary of Anne Frank* for a book report. I was concerned about her reading it because I was not sure I was ready to face questions about human cruelty beyond comprehension. However, after reading my daughter's report, I discovered she had no awareness of why the Franks were living in hiding. To her, Anne was any teenager who was having problems with her mother.

Also, don't criticize your daughter's literary tastes. Many adolescents have rather macabre interests and devour books such as *Sybil* (schizophrenia) or *Alive* (plane crash and cannibalism). Some teens will not read a book unless it is in paperback. Others are only interested in glamour magazines or diet books. Whatever your daughter gets out of reading is more than she would get if she did not read. Being supportive of what she reads and encouraging her to speak about it can develop the reading habit. An active campaign (mine lasted about two years) can pay off. You may not turn your daughter into an avid reader, but you can foster her looking through the daily newspapers or reading a book or magazine while traveling. You might even be fortunate enough to be able to replace your daughter's telephone time with reading.

HER SAVINGS

Generally, your daughter should be allowed to purchase what she wants with her money. Sometimes it is very difficult not to say anything though, when your family is worried about the mortgage payment and she comes home with an expensive camera. But, unless you told her the money was needed for the household or that you expected to borrow from her, don't get into an argument about her purchase. (If you borrow money from your daughter, pay it back as soon as you are able.) As long as it is her money and you do not need to use it, she should be allowed to do what she wants with it. Of course, you could mention that the item was a bad buy or that perhaps she should give some thought to why she feels she needs two cameras.

You should also try to limit the available cash your daughter has. For example, whenever my daughter's savings reach $700 or so, I strongly urge (insist!) that she invest $500 in a certificate of deposit. This way she is not tempted to overspend and she still has enough money to drive to Florida during a semester break.

6
IMPORTANT RELATIONSHIPS

COMPARISONS BETWEEN YOU AND HER

Almost every mother knows she should not make comparisons between her children—so much has been written or said about that topic. However, what hasn't been given enough attention is comparisons between mother and daughter.

When your daughter was little, she loved being told she was just like her mother. Now the same comment will make her cringe. The merest hint from you or someone else that she is similar to you will evoke expressions of disgust. Don't despair. You know you're not disgusting. Actually, your daughter's friends may think the way you look and act is okay. However, they are not your daughter.

Adolescent girls go through an intense negative phase where everything is magnified out of proportion. If you are slightly over-weight, your daughter views you as fat; if you still tease your hair, you're hopelessly old-fashioned about *everything*. Your daughter is simply unable to treat comparisons realistically, so don't let your feelings be hurt. Instead, smile through it and know that once she feels secure, she will be more than happy to be like you.

For example, my daughter is very much like me. Even her

junior-year term paper was the same topic that I had chosen in my junior year. When she told me of her choice I was really pleased—affirmation of self is always complimentary. However, I said nothing because at that time I knew nothing about anything, as far as she was concerned. If she knew I had chosen the same topic, she would have changed hers. At some point during her work on the paper I lost my ''dummy'' status for some inexplicable reason. I then told her I had done a similar report, and since I had now evolved into a semi-intelligent being, we were able to discuss the changes time had wrought on the topic. Had I told her earlier, she would have had to choose something different just to avoid being anything like me.

Wait for your daughter's distortions to smooth out. She will often want to be like you if it's her choice. In the meantime, don't make direct comparisons between her present self and you at her age. Also, don't try to look like her or dress like her when the two of you are together. You may like hearing how young you look—but what your daughter hears is how old and awful she looks.

If you happen to look a lot better than your daughter, and always will no matter what the ages, take care that your ''look'' is definitely more mature than hers. If you look so good, you shouldn't need to hear it at her expense, expecially when it's her school concert, or her party, or her graduation. Let her be the star she deserves to be. When she develops confidence in herself, she will be able to accept lots of stars in her life, including you.

IF SHE'S AN ONLY CHILD

Adolescence hits parents of only children like a ton of bricks. Suddenly their wonderful, cute, devoted, cooperative, well-mannered, well-spoken, happy daughter seems to short-circuit. Now she wants to dress her own way; she spends hours locked up by herself or with her friends, she is very secretive, she is barely civil to family visitors and relatives and, worst of all, she doesn't think you are so wonderful any more either.

It's enough to send the most understanding mother to the psychology books. Unless the mother of the only child has many families around where she can observe the capricious behavior of other teenagers, she is going to feel that something is wrong with her daughter. She has become so peculiar! Every stage in her development is new and unexpected.

Much of adolescent behavior is extreme. When your daughter refuses to talk to you or locks her bedroom door or begs not to be sent to the wonderful camp you have chosen, you wonder if someone, you or she, should be talking to a therapist. If she seems not to be happy about going on a trip or is happy tucked away with her tapes, gerbils and French summer assignment, don't be too concerned. Most likely the answer is just to relax and stop pushing so hard. Being expected to be perfect or to overachieve is probably a special burden of an only child. Your daughter is retrenching for her passage from adolescence to maturity. She has had the benefit of lots of attention from you through the years, and as long as she continues to feel your love and concern, she will make a safe passage. It's helpful to you, of course, if you put yourself in touch with other mothers of teenagers, mostly to allay your own fears.

Adolescence is the time for your daughter to separate from you so that she can find out who she is and then be that person. Too much intervention on your part is going to slow the separation process and make the atmosphere in your home unnecessarily stormy. It is often more difficult for the only child to separate because there are no other children around for her parents to focus on. This may be a good time for *you* to develop other interests—perhaps start a new business or begin graduate school.

SIBLINGS

Even when your children are close in age or of the same sex, they should be treated as individuals. What you do for one, you need not do for the other. Explain that, as a parent, your job is to see that each child's needs are met. Buying a guitar for Alice, who is interested in music, does not mean you need to buy a guitar for tone-deaf Sue. As a matter of fact, you need not buy anything for Sue until she has her own special need.

If your teen daughter accuses you of favoring her brother or sister over her, explain you are only human and it is perfectly natural that at certain times you will like one child better than the other, just as sometimes you prefer cake over ice cream. Nobody can like or treat their children exactly the same way even some of the time, because no two people are alike. Also, tell her that you could not be exactly the same from moment to moment even if you tried. Remind her about the youngster she sits for who wants to hear the bedtime story told *exactly* the way she told it before. She knows how impossible it is to do that.

Remember not to act as a referee if your children quarrel. You cannot win. Let them work it out for themselves as long as no blows are struck. If physical fighting does occur, intervene to stop the fighting but do not take sides. If one always gets the better of the other, speak to each child in private. It takes two to make a disagreement. Don't automatically favor the "loser." It may be that the "weaker" one uses his or her vulnerability to get your attention. If your children are always at each other and often come to blows, or if one consistently takes advantage of the other, some change in the family's routine is necessary. Seek outside counseling for advice.

Take care not to create a rift between your children because of your perception of justness. It is healthier for them to be in cahoots against you than against each other. Allow them to stand together and "pull the wool over your eyes" occasionally. Siblings are often so different that the only bond between them is their parents. Be careful not to destroy what your children's only commonality may be. Don't set one against the other. Don't force one to tattle on the other and don't listen to any tattling. (Of course, if you suspect a serious problem, like drugs or stealing, explain to the uninvolved child that responding to your questions is not tattling, but really helping the troubled child.)

FATHERS, STEPFATHERS AND VISITING FATHERS

You are a mother, not a martyr, referee or saint. Assuming your husband is not a fiend or child molester, you should not interfere in conflicts between your daughter and her father. (This is true even if your husband is not your daughter's natural father.) Obviously, there will be times when you feel you must say something, but avoid taking sides. Of course it's fine to support your daughter during a conflict if your help and advice were enlisted from the beginning, but avoid jumping in in the middle of a clash. Generally, it's better to go to a movie and hear about it later. If you are asked to take sides, don't. Simple responses such as "It's just a phase she's going through," to your husband, or "Who said life is fair?" to your daughter, should suffice.

It may be, however, that her father is so adoring (either because of, or in spite of, his feelings toward you) that he spoils her unnecessarily and overtly favors her over you or the other children. This is especially common with divorced fathers who see their daughters only on weekends or during the summer. It's hard for them not to play superpop. As a result you wind up being the "heavy," especially if you work. What usually happens is that on "his" weekends, she has no responsibility. On "your" weekends, you either pile on the chores or supervise the completion of school projects. However, it's not necessary for you to be the mean one to counterbalance the father's actions. That's not fair to you or your daughter. You're entitled to your own relationship, not one that is merely a response to the relationship between your daughter and her father. Speak to her father. Perhaps he can drive her to the orthodontist on his weekends, or scour the libraries with her for a book on medieval witchcraft. You are entitled to some time to spoil your daughter too.

On the other hand, your daughter's father may be unduly harsh or strict. If so, try to change his mind, but do so in private. However, if his beliefs and actions are truly out of step with reality and he refuses to bend, seek outside advice.

Remember, too, that some adolescent girls like to think of their father as The Great Protector. Your daughter may say things like "You know how Daddy feels about boys [or staying out late, or drinking]." She likes the idea that her father is there as nay-sayer at a time when she is not ready to join the activities of her friends. It gives her an excuse not to take risks she's not ready to take. However, make sure that your daughter knows that her father is not her only protector. Sometimes you must be the one to lay down the law. You don't want her to feel she always has to look to a male for protection. She needs to learn that women, too, are capable of protecting each other and themselves.

LIFE WITH FATHER

If your daughter threatens, "I'll move to Daddy's if you don't let me go to Louise's party," explain that she can move to her father's any time she wants, but she still can't go to Louise's party. While she may jump at the idea of living with her father, let her know that changing households is a major decision and she cannot flit from one to the other just because she thinks she will have fewer chores or a later curfew. Also, it may dampen your daughter's enthusiasm for a move when you point out that her father is allergic to her cats and that she will have to train him to put up with her loud noises, telephone calls and organic diet. Adolescents can be extremely practical. When given respect and a careful look at the options before her, your daughter will probably decide on the status quo.

Sometimes, though, the tension between you and your daughter may reach a point that is intolerable. You and she simply cannot coexist at even the most basic level of civility. There are constant differences of opinion, spiteful actions by both and, worse, self-destructive acts on your daughter's part. Don't be afraid or embarrassed to consider alternative living arrangements for your daughter. If you are divorced and she has a good relationship with her father, she could live with him. (If there's no divorced father for her to live with, consider allowing her to live with friends or relatives. Boarding school might also be a solution.)

If you and your daughter don't get along, don't feel you have failed as a mother. You and she simply have a problem living together. Many people can't live together. Sometimes counseling can help. However, often the solution is for mother and daughter to live apart. But remember, living apart may give you and your daughter a chance for a warm, loving relationship. Don't maintain a stormy relationship because of false pride or your insecurity. You want your daughter to be able to develop herself. She cannot do that in an environment where she directs most of her energies toward taunting you.

HER STEPMOTHER

If your daughter likes her stepmother, consider it to your credit. If she did not think too much of mothers she would be unlikely to think too much of stepmothers. If one mother is a good thing, two must be better!

If your daughter really dislikes her stepmother, it may be that she is having problems letting go of her fantasies about her father or is still resentful about the divorce. Try to get her to understand that it may not be the stepmother who is the problem, but the situation. This will probably turn out to be another one-sided talk. You throw out ideas and she shrugs, grunts, hollers *"Mother!"* or leaves the room. However, continue on with your thoughtful monologue. Sooner or later something you say will hit home—and she will hear it, if not discuss it.

If your daughter thinks her stepmother is wonderful, do not feel jealous or slighted. She might really be a super-terrific person. Worse, she may even be younger, more talented, better looking or more successful than you. You need not worry that you will appear less in your daughter's eyes. She will compare her stepmother to her friends' stepmothers, not to you. She knows the difference between a stepmother and a mother. You may think your daughter's friends are terrific, but honestly, would you really want any one of them to be your daughter instead of your own? Your daughter's raving about her wonderful stepmother is no different from her carrying on about a favored teacher or a movie star.

If the stepmother's values are different from yours, let them be so. Your daughter's not a two-year-old who needs special feeding and care. Consider the differences as part of her overall education—the world is full of different people who do things differently, and different is not synonymous with better or worse.

APPEARING WITH HER STEPMOTHER

Your young teen daughter will go through a sickeningly "cute" phase. She will dress in pink and adorn her room with stuffed animals. She will squeal at teenage rock stars and offer to do the dishes. She will also want you to appear together with daddy and stepmommy at public functions.

It's not that you dislike your ex-husband's new wife. You just feel awkward, especially if you have not remarried. Also, why should *she* be there and share the kudos? She didn't raise your daughter—your did, and you want the glory. You're the one who suffered through the homework so she could graduate junior high with honors, or chauffeured her to spelling bees or to special instructions for her confirmation or dance recital. It's okay that her father will be there—after all, he is her father.

However, you feel foolish and petty explaining all this to your daughter. She has been so sweet and thoughtful lately, and you don't want to disappoint her.

Honesty is best. Try to ascertain whether or not you will actually feel uncomfortable or whether you are concerned with what others will think. You may find that after analyzing your own feelings you wouldn't mind appearing with your ex-husband and his second wife. You might even welcome the opportunity to show how civilized and sophisticated you are. On the other hand, if the thought of a combined appearance makes you miserable, don't threaten, "If *she* goes, I won't." It's unfair for your daughter to have to choose. Instead, let her know how you feel. If you decide to go, even if you don't really want to, it doesn't hurt for your daughter to know you're doing something for her. You need not be a martyr about it or make her feel guilty. If handled right, you will at least feel altruistic and your daughter will know you really care about her feelings.

If you do go, appear together with your ex-husband and his new wife. It would be wrong to force your daughter to choose between two sides of the auditorium after her appearance. Furthermore, you would feel hurt because chances are she would pick her father's side. You've brought her up to be polite, and the stepmother would deserve "guest treatment." Remember, she

104

probably feels more secure about your feelings toward her than anyone else's, and as a result takes you for granted.

If you can't bring yourself to go to the event, your daughter will probably be disappointed. However, explain that you have a right not to be perfect (just as she has) and that even people who love each other sometimes disappoint each other. The important thing to remember in this instance is that it's your problem, not your daughter's, and you shouldn't make her feel guilty for wanting everything just right.

YOU AS A STEPMOTHER

Be yourself. See yourself as any mother and be guided by the advice and principles in this book. Don't be apologetic or defensive. Treat your stepdaughter as you would your own daughter—with love, patience and respect.

If your stepdaughter is visiting you for the first time, of course it is natural to treat her like a guest. Thereafter, though, just treat her as "special" as we all are special people, not special because she is "stepdaughter special." Also, if she wants to treat you as a friend, that's fine, but don't become so friendly that you lose all right to authority. You should not usurp her natural parents, but if, for example, she asks to go out and you are in charge, answer according to your own judgment rather than make no decision.

If your stepdaughter is hostile toward you, don't be taken aback. It is likely she is feeling hostile toward her natural mother or father as well. Give the relationship time. She needs to come to grips with reality, and your adding to her problems by insisting on friendliness will not dispel the hostility. You can demand civil treatment and respect, but not friendship or affection. If you are patient and do nothing to polarize the situation, she should come around.

However, it may be that there will never be any deep feeling or caring between the two of you. She may just not be able to develop a warm, loving relationship with you or vice versa. You may not even like each other, which is a very real possibility if you came on the scene when she was entering her teens. However, if you behave as the adult, a relationship based on mutual respect, if not affection, should develop.

If a serious problem arises with your stepdaughter about her behavior or concerning a major decision that has to be made which will affect her life, stay out of it. Her natural parents must deal with it. Don't volunteer your opinion even if you feel it's a waste of money to send her to an expensive college when she's a poor student. At best you will be accused of meddling; at worst, of being selfish. If your husband is distraught about the matter, be understanding and a good listener. Realize, though, that it is his problem, not yours.

RELATIVES

If a confrontation arises between your mother and your daughter and you can't stay out of it, support your daughter. After all, your mother's already grown-up but your daughter needs to know that she can trust you. For example, my mother had accepted a dinner invitation for us which my daughter did not wish to honor. She had no homework or other plans. She simply did not want to go because she would be bored. My mother was aghast. How could I let my daughter disobey her? What would her friends think? How could she face them, knowing that her granddaughter didn't want to go with her? A big disagreement developed and I supported my daughter's right to choose. Surprisingly, the results benefited all. I felt good about standing up to my own mother, my mother had more respect for me as an adult, and my daughter was assured that I was on her side. (I told her later she owed me one!)

Whether or not your daughter needs to be on hand when relatives or friends arrive, or to stay around to entertain the cousins, should depend on the particular situation. Let your daughter know who's coming and when, and what you would like her to do. For example, Aunt Emma and Uncle Charlie are coming to dinner. It would be nice for your daughter to be present for dinner, but she needn't stay home the entire evening. If Aunt and Uncle are bringing six-year-old Tracy and you all are planning to go out after dinner, ask your daughter to sit. If she can't or won't, don't force her. Hire a babysitter. Of course, you should be more demanding if they are coming in to visit Great Uncle Harry in the hospital. However, even then, if your daughter has made plans already, hire a sitter. Don't assume that your needs or good times always come ahead of your daughter's. She is part of other people's plans and when she cancels out, others may need to change their plans, too. If you think it's going to be a long evening and you would like your daughter around, ask her to invite a friend to dinner and to sleep over. If teenage cousins have been dragged along by Aunt and Uncle, they may or may not want to go out with your daughter. They probably feel awkward themselves and would like to interfere in your daughter's life as little as possible. Let them work it out but don't feel your daughter's rude if she goes out and the cousins stay home. They may all feel more comfortable that way.

Don't force your daughter to go visiting with you unless it's a special occasion like a wedding or Aunt Matilda's 102nd birthday. There probably is nothing for her to do. If possible, and time and distance permit, it should be okay for her to come along, make an appearance and then leave with the excuse that it's a school night. Remember, too, when you need to apologize for your daughter's absence, to make the same social excuses for her as you would for anyone else. Just say she had a babysitting job or a school paper to do but otherwise she would have loved to come. Your hosts have a right to expect politeness from you and it certainly is not going to make them feel good if you tell them that your daughter thinks they're stiffs.

Sometimes visiting relatives is a duty, sometimes it is fun. You shouldn't expect your daughter to have the same duties as you or to think the same people are fun. If you treat the situation fairly, you will find her cooperative when you need her to be around. You never know, she may want to be around when you least expect her to.

FRIENDS

HERS. Your daughter's friends are her friends, not yours. You don't need to like them. Most likely you will like only one, and find the others either too sneaky, too timid, too bossy or too wild. However, don't interfere in any relationships that your daughter has with boys or girls unless it is obvious that the relationship is destructive. For example, you may notice that your daughter always does what Beth wants, or that she is upset when she comes home from an evening with her friends. These are instances when words alone are insufficient and you need to support them with action.

If you feel the relationship with Beth is harmful, and your daughter complains that "Beth never wants to go anywhere . . . all we do is walk around town . . . Beth won't even go bowling with me," telling your daughter to stand up for herself will not enable her to do it. She may be able to in a few years, but right now you want to be sure she doesn't get down on herself and become even less confident. Just telling her to find new friends is pointless, because that's not so easy to do.

Perhaps you can find a bowling league for her to join. She may protest, but don't be surprised to hear her tell Beth that she *has* to join because her mother insists. If you get her to go, she will find new friends and Beth will either join her or drop from the scene. (If your daughter refuses to go to the league, she is probably just as content as Beth to "hang around" but doesn't want to admit that to you or herself. If she and Beth are happy and neither is troublesome, just boring for the moment, one of them will outgrow the other sooner or later. Just continue nagging for now so you won't be deficient in your role as mother.)

If you suspect your daughter is being pressured into sex or drugs or alcohol by her peers, see if you can involve her more in home activities. Remember, mothers are marvelous scapegoats. Do not be afraid to pull in the reins if she seems to be losing her way. Pay her to do the laundry, or *need* her to take care of her brothers and sisters. Spend a few weekends camping. Do something to break her old routine. Help her to become involved in a constructive time-consuming activity. Perhaps she can be encouraged to commit herself to working to improve the environment or find a part-time job. Help her to change her daily patterns even if it stretches your budget to the utmost and makes extra demands on your time. If your efforts are unsuccessful and your daughter goes back to her old ways, get outside help. Don't wait until it is too late. Beware of the temptation to blame your daughter's bad behavior on her friends. Remember, your daughter is the one with the problem and it does not matter whether the cause of the problem began because of her weakness or at the instigation of her friends.

YOURS. Your daughter doesn't expect you to socialize with or pass judgment on her friends. You shouldn't expect her to pass judgment or socialize with your friends either. When your friends visit, she should, of course, be polite and make them comfortable until you can be with them, just as you do when her friends arrive. However, she should not be forced to stay around. Naturally you want to show her off, but how would you feel if you were forced to sit and listen to her and her friends squeal about the latest television stars, or how tough a marker the new English teacher is. I'm sure she'd find your conversation equally boring. Besides, sometimes it's more fun to eavesdrop than to be a participant.

If she wants to join you, and your friends have no objection, that's fine *sometimes*. She may want to be with you and your friends because she is under a lot of pressure. Being with adults for a short time can give her a chance to relax and recharge herself. It's not fine, though, if she seems to prefer adult company most of the time. Try to find out whether she's having problems with her friends.

If you are single and date, do not regard each and every beau as a potential stepfather. Your daughter should join you only after you and he have known each other for a while, and then only occasionally. Of course, some situations call for "family fun" such as a day at the beach. However, even on such occasions, if your daughter joins you, ask her to bring a girl friend along. She shouldn't bring a boy friend unless they have a long-standing relationship. Otherwise, don't double-date with your daughter.

Also, don't invite comments about your dates or let your date get too chummy with your daughter. She has no rights with respect to whom you do or don't get involved with. Keep your relationships with men casual as far as your daughter is concerned. Otherwise, you will find you have placed yourself in an awkward position when you stop dating a particular man. She may experience separation anxiety when you stop dating that person. She may see the end of your relationship as a rejection of her.

7
POTENTIAL PROBLEMS

SEX

"IT'S TIME WE HAD A TALK"

These days everyone says that parents should discuss sex with their children. Have you ever tried to? It seems that as far as adolescent girls are concerned, sex may be for the birds and bees but it is not for their parents. Adolescent fantasies go as far as graduation or marriage. All life stops then. Therefore, how could you know anything about sex? You're middle-aged—too old to have sexual desires and even well beyond the memory of any!

If the criterion for being a modern parent is to openly discuss sex with one's children, I have failed miserably. My daughter would never let me discuss sex with her. Even letters (which I thought were potential Pulitzer winners) sent to her at camp were mysteriously never received—only food and money got through. The most I have managed is as follows.

Phase I—when she was eleven.

> ME: Now that you may soon become a woman, there are a few things we should discuss . . .
> SHE: (Bored expression.)

ME: Seriously . . . we need to talk about a few things.
SHE: I know everything.
ME: Sex? Babies? Intercourse? Contraception? Disease?
SHE: *Mother!* (Slams door and turns on radio.)

Variations of the above were repeated every six months or so until Phase II—when she was around fifteen.

ME: Now that you'll be going out with boys who have cars, there are a few things we should discuss . . .
SHE: I don't want a lecture.
ME: No lecture, honey. I just want to make sure you know that boys and girls view things differently.
SHE: *MOTHER!* (Leaves room to blow-dry hair.)

Phase III—at around age seventeen.

SHE: I'm going to the beach.
ME: With who?
SHE: Jerry, from history class—his father has a house at the beach.
ME: Just the two of you?
SHE: No, his brother will be there.
ME: How old is his brother?
SHE: Twenty.
ME: (Puzzled . . . do I discuss a ménage à trois?) Honey, there are a few things we should discuss . . .
SHE: But Jerry and I are friends.
ME: True, but sea, sun and sand have made lots of lovers out of friends.
SHE: *MOTHER!* (Disappears to find sun-tan lotion.)

Phase IV—when she's home for a semester break from college.

SHE: I need a pretty bra.

Even though I failed as a "modern parent," I guess I have been successful in getting some messages across about sex and contraception, because as far as I know my daughter has been sexually responsible throughout her teen years. She has more or less adopted my standards. For example, the Kinsey studies showed that most young women become sexually active about five years after menstruating regularly. That seems a reasonable time span to me. I feel it would be unfair to expect a young woman who has had adult sexual feelings since the age of eleven to respond and feel at age fifteen the same way as a teen who had just begun menstruating at that age.

Try to impart your standards and values to your daughter, but don't feel you have failed to give her a sex education if your attempts to discuss it have been futile. It is not discussions about sex that control your daughter's sexual activity, but how she views herself and you. A teenage girl who is secure about herself will be less vulnerable to pressure from her dates. However, you must be realistic. You must realize that your daughter may become curious or be overwhelmed by desire—either sexual or the wish to be popular. Or she may be too timid to be assertive enough to say no. There's also the possibility that she may believe differently than you. Therefore, you must make sure she knows about contraception and venereal disease even if you believe that women should be virgins when they marry. Her virginity is her decision—you won't be there to decide for her. Your responsibility is to see that she has the information and maturity to make such a decision wisely and carefully. You needn't rush the topic, though, by launching into a discussion of herpes-2 the first time your twelve-year-old walks home from a party with a boy. But don't close your eyes to the possibility that your fifteen-year-old daughter may engage in sex. Look and listen for cues so you can make sure she has whatever information she needs when she needs it. As I said, a face-to-face discussion is not the only way. You or your daughter may be too embarrassed. Such discussions may need to be held with a wall between the two of you, or you may want to write her a letter. You could even leave informative pamphlets on her dresser or ask her doctor to speak to her the next time she visits.

Some parents are permitted to talk about all aspects of sex with their daughters. Their daughters come home and tell them that they are frustrated and that they can't wait until they're old enough to try it out. They talk openly about the latest in contraception and feminine hygiene. (I've gotten as far as telling my daughter the location of a nearby teenage health clinic and recommending yoghurt.) I think that's terrific. I would love to be able to talk to my daughter about love and feelings. I would like her to know how I feel about sexual intimacy and responsibility, but she has never asked. It's definitely easier if your daughter asks questions. Don't be afraid to answer them. For example, the daughter of a friend of mine asked her about oral sex. My friend's response was simple and delicate: "When you love someone, every part of their body is beautiful." Another friend was asked by her college-age daughter about having an affair with more than one boy at a time. My friend was floored at first, but she didn't want to condemn or condone. Her response was perfect: "One *might* be okay, but two or three—you won't get your homework done!"

PREGNANCY

So many times your daughter has said, "I've got to tell you something. Promise you won't be mad?" So many times you have promised over and over that you wouldn't be mad. In the past, fortunately, the news has been nothing more than an F in physics or a scratched car fender. This time, though, through tears and quivering lips, she tells you she's pregnant. You are stunned. How could this happen? She's only fourteen . . . or she's seventeen and should know better. After the initial shock, you become angry. How could she do this to you!

Look at the bright side. Pregnancy is not a fatal disease nor is it addictive. Your daughter made a serious error in judgment. Being pregnant as a teen is definitely unfortunate, but *it is not a tragedy*. Since your daughter told you of her condition, she obviously wants your help and advice. Try to be objective and rational and discuss the options open to her. Don't focus on why or how she got pregnant. Deal with the present problem—her pregnancy. This is not the time to lay a guilt trip on her or yourself.

The solution has to be *her* decision, even if she opts for an abortion. Remember, you do not have the right to force her to have an abortion; you should, therefore, not have the right to prevent her from having one. Help your daughter decide what is best for her. Ask her doctor for all relevant information, but keep in mind it is not the doctor's decision but your daughter's. Basically, she has four choices.

1. Getting Married and Keeping the Baby. Marriage is feasible only if an older teen is involved and the prospective parents planned to marry anyway. Even then, unless both sets of future in-laws are prepared to support the newlyweds emotionally and financially (assuming the father-to-be is also a teen), marriage is not a wise solution. For example, if my daughter chose marriage in this situation, I would continue to support her as if she were still attending school and, in fact, do everything I could to help her to continue her studies as soon as possible. I would expect the boy's parents to do the same for their son. There is no reason to punish the children by requiring them to quit school and materially alter the course of their lives. Adjusting to marriage and a baby is difficult enough. Don't make it more difficult by withdrawing your support and forcing them to be instant adults—"You made your bed, now lie in it." Criminals get off with lighter sentences.

2. Giving Birth and Keeping the Baby as an Unwed Mother. This solution is feasible only if you (or an understanding friend or relative) live in an area where no stigma is attached to having a child out of wedlock and where flexible infant care, school and work schedules could be arranged. If this solution is chosen, be positive. Start thinking of and referring to your daughter as a "single parent" rather than as an unwed mother. She could use a little self-image bolstering.

3. Giving Birth and Putting the Baby Up for Adoption. Community values and family finances play an important part in reaching this decision. You may live in an area that ostracizes "fallen women," or perhaps your family simply cannot afford to care for a baby or support your daughter during the early years of a teen marriage. If this solution is chosen, consider whether your daughter would be able to live at home and continue school during her pregnancy or whether she would need to leave town to stay with "sick Aunt Louise." Consider also what she would return to. Would the community reject her? Would such rejection cause her to turn to drugs or become promiscuous? Make sure your daughter understands what she may have to face *after* she gives birth. If she knows beforehand that it will be difficult because everyone in town is unlikely to forget her mistake soon, it will be easier for her to handle her return. In some instances it might be wiser for her to stay with Aunt Louise permanently.

4. Having an Abortion. Abortion is probably the most unpleasant choice. However, if my daughter chose to have an abortion, I would support her decision. After all, it is her body and her life. Frankly, if she were a young teen, I would even urge an abortion, because giving birth at a young age is dangerous for the mother-to-be and the unborn infant.

Your feelings and solutions may be different or similar to mine. That is not important. What is important is that you answer your daughter's call for help and help in the way that is best for her. How strongly you push for one solution over another depends, of course, a great deal on your daughter's age and ambitions. Obviously, your input should be stronger the younger she is.

Whatever option is chosen, make sure your daughter at least finishes high school. If your community is unresponsive to her plight, perhaps she can live with friends or relatives until she finishes school. If you have no such relatives or friends and an abortion is out of the question, ask your daughter's doctor for information about where she can stay during her pregnancy and finish her education.

PROMISCUITY

You suspect your daughter is promiscuous. If you confront her with your suspicions, she will either deny it or flaunt it. I doubt that she will say, "Oh, Mommy, you are right. Help me."

Your daughter's promiscuity probably stems from a lack of self-respect. Use a little subterfuge. There must be other areas where it is apparent that she doesn't stand up for herself or think much of herself. She may need constant assurance or acceptance from her friends. Perhaps she gives away her prized possessions so people will like her. Use these behavioral traits as a basis to discuss her getting professional help.

Your daughter may have some very real hesitations about your knowing how far she has gone sexually. Remember, in our society, sex is still a very private matter. Respect your daughter's privacy. Let her retain some pride and don't cross-examine her about her sexual activity. If she is promiscuous, she does need professional help. Your job is to lead her to help, not to punish her or be a voyeur.

HOMOSEXUALITY

If you have reason to suspect your daughter is a lesbian, seek professional counseling. However, don't assume she is a lesbian if as an early adolescent she has crushes on older women or spends a lot of time behind closed doors with the same girl friend. Young adolescent girls tend to be close with one another. They brush each other's hair, whisper into each other's ears, follow each other into the bathroom.

A good rule of thumb as to what constitutes lesbian behavior is your instinct. If something about the way your daughter and her girl friend behave makes you uneasy, some deviant activity probably is going on. You know your daughter, and just as your instincts tell you when she's coming down with a cold or when she's not telling you the whole story, there's no reason to discount your instincts now.

However, even if some sexual activity is going on between your young daughter and a girl friend, that does not mean all hell need break loose. Intervene into the relationship tactfully. Find reasons for no more sleepovers. Be at home when the other girl visits. Speak to your daughter about lesbianism without personalizing it or making her feel guilty. (Who knows, maybe female adolescent closeness is a carryover from our primate ancestors who constantly groomed one another.) Simply say that our society does not accept any sexual behavior between members of the same sex. Inform your daughter that some girls have the need to express themselves physically before they are ready for a male-female relationship, because they may feel unloved or unaccepted at home. Tell her you hope she knows how much you love her. Your explanation may need to be given through closed doors or by letter. Adolescents are often uncomfortable about any discussion having anything to do with sex or their bodies.

By the time your daughter is into her teens, she should have broken out of her intensely close relationship with any girl friend. That doesn't mean she and her friend will not still do each other's hair or speak to one another ten times a day on the telephone. What it does mean is that the relationship should be looking out instead of in. There should be some interest in boys—even if they are dismissed with an "ughh." Your daughter and her friend should be looking to meet new people and trying new things. If your daughter is around fourteen and still has just one or two friends who never go anywhere or participate in any after-school activities, *and* you feel a certain uneasiness, it would be wise to discuss your feelings with a professional to see if anything need be done.

If your daughter is going away to camp or to school, let her know about the possibility of advances from other girls or women. Don't frighten or disgust her. It's natural for you to let your daughter know of any kind of possible threat. Telling her that a female may make a pass at her should be no different than telling her that a male may, or telling her not to swim after eating, or to stay in one place if she gets lost in the woods. You owe it to your daughter to let her know of the existence of lesbianism even if she and you are embarrassed about discussing it.

PORNOGRAPHY

The problem with pornography is not so much that most of it is obscene but that it depicts women in a servile or passive state. As a woman, you should be against anything that connects eroticism to servility or passivity. However, you cannot forbid your daughter to read pornographic magazines or books or to see "porno flicks" any more than you can forbid anything else. In reality, you cannot prevent your daughter from doing what she wants to do outside the home, or even in the home when you are not there. The only thing that controls her behavior is her own self-discipline. Instead of forbidding, tell her your feelings and trust she will act accordingly.

If you suspect that what your daughter is seeing or reading is beyond her years or pornographic, tactfully introduce topics into your daily chatter to counterbalance what you perceive as too advanced for her. For example, if your daughter is reading an "adult" book and seems to be bothered by lurid descriptions of deviant sexual intercourse, keep your discussions simple and matter-of-fact. Explain that different people do different things. What you want to do is to relieve her fear that when she grows up she will do "disgusting" things. Impress on her that she always has the right to say no. You need to tread very carefully and not put down all unusual behavior as deviant. It may be that when your daughter becomes sexually active, she will be able to enjoy intercourse only if there are green lights on and the stereo is playing loudly. You don't want her to feel that oddities which cause no harm to her or anyone else are wrong or immoral.

Stick to the theme that men or women who participate in obscene or pornographic acts—those acts which are physically harmful or force one to be subservient to another—never learned to like themselves. Explain further that lots of people feel like or dream about doing something obscene, but just as some people think about poisoning their neighbor, feeling and thinking is not the same as doing. Reassure your daughter that just as she is not going to kill somebody simply because she has read a few murder mysteries, she is not going to become involved in obscene acts just because she has read about them or thinks about them occasionally.

YOUR SEXUALITY

Teens generally give very little thought to what their parents or any adults do. They are much too concerned with themselves. To them, as long as all is well, parents and adults are just mechanical beings who go to work, cook, clean house, watch television, never have any fun. Teens believe being "turned on" sexually is their own special domain and they cannot conceive of an adult being sexually excited. It's too gross . . . look at that man's beer belly, that lady's varicose veins. I know young teen girls who, despite their seeming sophistication about sex and contraception, believe parental sex is not ''sex'' but intercourse for the purpose of having a baby. If there are three children in the family, there were three acts of intercourse. It does not occur to them to wonder why their parents share a bedroom or a bed.

Adolescents especially do not like to think of their mothers as sexual persons. Walking in on you and your boy friend or you and your husband is going to shock your daughter into recognizing your sexuality. Don't assume that because she claims to know all about sex she won't be bothered by the realization that you engage in sex. If she just appears embarrassed by the incident, don't make an issue of it. She may be more mature than you think. If, however, she accuses you of being disgusting or thereafter treats you with hostility, you will need to go on a fishing expedition as soon as the two of you have some privacy. Was she embarrassed for you or for herself? Does she think sex is revolting? Or only your engaging in it? Is she jealous that you have a boy friend and she doesn't? Does she have a crush on your boy friend? Does she still retain the little-girl fantasy that she's going to marry her father when she grows up? Try to get her to talk about her feelings and respond accordingly.

There is, however, no reason for your daughter to find a strange man in your bed or on your couch. She has a right to know who is going to spend the night in her house. It is more than awkward for her to run into the living room in her underwear and find a snoring male on the sofa. At the least, it's inconsiderate behavior on your part. Absent a snowstorm or a visit from someone living out of town, your dates should not stay overnight. You don't want to give your daughter the impression that men come and go, that they function in your world only as sex objects.

Having your steady boy friend stay overnight or live in should not threaten your daughter as long as she has met him and knows of your plans in advance. You need not go into detail about your relationship, nor ask her permission. Simply say, ''You know John . . . he's moving in. We've decided we really care about each other and want to spend as much time together as possible.'' Assure her that his moving in will not intrude on her privacy. She need not give up her room or change her shower schedule. You might also want to let her know that you will have more time for her because you will be going out less often. Of course, this may be the last thing she wants to hear!

TODAY'S DANGERS

DRUGS

Drug addiction is a problem for which professional help should be sought immediately. If you suspect that your daughter is addicted, confront her for affirmation and go from there. If she either denies the addiction or refuses your help, *you* should seek professional help as to what your next step should be. Be prepared to change your daughter's school or to move, if necessary.

However, occasional drug use is not the same as addiction, and if you find your daughter is an occasional user, your response should be appropriate to the situation. It's probably the rare teenager today who has not had at least a puff of a marijuana cigarette. Personally, I completely disapprove of any drug use because drugs scare me, but realistically, six kids sharing a joint at a Saturday-night party is not going to turn your daughter into a junkie. What will, though, is a low opinion of herself. Be careful to treat your daughter with respect and as a worthwhile and useful human being. Her having a positive attitude about herself will go a lot further in preventing drug addiction than any lecture you can give her.

Look at any situation involving drugs and your daughter as objectively as possible and be as concrete as possible. For example, when my daughters were pubescent, my fear was not that they would become addicted to drugs, but that someone would give them something too strong for them and they would die of an overdose. There was a nine-year-old pusher at the elementary school who gave some "uppers" to a few eleven-year-old girls. One of the girls had a six-year-old brother to whom she gave one of the pills. He went into a coma. Therefore, I told my children, at every opportunity, never to take anything given to them—at least until they had passed puberty. I instilled in them the fear that because their bodies were going through so many changes, a pill that might seem fun to one person could be fatal to another. No one could foresee the result of one's individual chemistry mixing with a drug. Even doctors prescribe medication by the weight and age of the patient.

When discussing the harmful effects of drugs, you too should personalize your examples. Remember, children are so now-oriented that anything said in the abstract is not absorbed. When stating that drugs can do harmful things to a person's body, remind your daughter about the time Uncle Harry went into shock from penicillin, or about the severe headaches you get from over-the-counter diet pills, or how the whole world can take Alka-Seltzer except her. When she realizes that everyday drugs can have disastrous effects, the dangers of taking an unknown quantity of an unknown drug will be more real to her. Counter your daughter's "marijuana is not harmful" argument by simply stating the obvious. Marijuana is illegal. Why does she want to line the pockets of criminals and risk jail herself while they go free? Also, be absolutely adamant about the danger of mixing any drugs and alcohol or driving while under the influence of drugs. Tell her that there is no "high" worth dying for.

The "addiction in any form is harmful" argument is also a powerful tool. For example, your daughter confronts you with an article that says smoking marijuana is beneficial. I see no point in getting into a no-win situation about the pros and cons of marijuana smoking. Instead, respond simply that in certain circumstances it may not be harmful, but addiction *in any form* is. It doesn't matter what the addiction is. Anyone who must do or have something that society frowns upon has a problem. Tell her that if she, or anyone she knows, must take drugs to get through an exam or go to a party, that person has a problem. Suggest she would be doing that person a real favor by assisting them in getting help.

This is not what your daughter expects to hear. She is prepared with only the pros and cons of using drugs, and is hoping to get your back-door approval of her behavior. However, use is not the issue, addiction is. She knows you don't want her to be a user. You've told her a thousand times. However, whether she uses or will use drugs is solely in her control. Your goal, if you have not been able to discourage all drug use, is to get her to monitor herself, or in other words, to think for herself.

I'm not advocating acceptance of drug use. Instead, make sure your daughter is aware of the dangers of even sporadic use, but direct your discussions toward addiction. You want to keep the channels open so she can come to you and mention that she has "tried" drugs without your rushing to call the police. Listen carefully to see if she is signaling you to intervene. You want her to be able to come to you for help. You want her to know when she is out of control. What you want her to do in that event is to come to you—not be too ashamed or frightened to face you with her problem.

ALCOHOL

While your daughter is not likely to die from drinking alcohol, the possibility that she might be killed by a drunk driver is far too real. You can give her a fairly free reign on the issue of dating and curfews but you should make her swear on a stack of Rolling Stones albums that she will never go in a car with a driver who is even slightly drunk; that she will instead call to be picked up, no matter where she is, how late the hour, or what she may have been doing. Get your point across. This is the type of situation in which you should exercise your parental authority loudly and convincingly.

Your daughter's drinking is a different situation. Some adolescents get drunk with their friends just to see what it's like. Often it is the result of simple curiosity, like the nine-year-old who threw tomatoes and eggs from a third-floor window to see them go splat. When she was nine, she did not realize she could hurt someone by her prank; at twelve or thirteen, she is oblivious to the fact that alcohol could hurt *her*. If something like that happens involving your daughter, and all else seems in order, don't be too concerned. Move the liquor to a less obvious place. Leave your daughter alone for shorter periods of time for a while, but do so tactfully. Don't give her the impression that you don't trust her. Treat it simply as something foolish that she did. However, if this situation has occurred more than once, or if you have reason to suspect that she is drinking more than a beer or two at a Saturday-night party, face the issue squarely. It may be she has a personal problem or that she needs a new group of friends. Depending on the situation, seek outside advice, or perhaps extracurricular activities or a job would be the answer. Sometimes a more drastic step such as a change of school or neighborhood is required.

Whether or not you let your daughter drink at home is your own business. Some people advocate that children should be taught to drink at home; others say parents who drink even socially at home set a bad example. You don't need to serve your daughter a drink, though, just because you're having one. As an adult you have certain privileges that your minor daughter does not have—you can see X-rated movies, drink in bars, vote, take out a loan. If, however, you serve wine at dinner and your daughter joins you, she's not going to become an alcoholic as a result (assuming, of course, that you are not an alcoholic and you and your daughter do not join each other for martinis every night).

Remember, however, that while you do have the right to serve alcohol to your daughter, you do not have the right to serve it to her friends. Perhaps parents wouldn't object if their daughter was served a little wine at dinner or some champagne on a special occasion. They don't, however, expect their fourteen-year-old to go to a party where beer is flowing, provided by the host parents, nor do they expect their sixteen-year-old to be served hard liquor by her friends' parents. Unless you know the family, when in doubt, don't offer.

Sometimes, though, your daughter will place you in an awkward situation. You will need to relax your standards a little to avoid embarrassing her. For example, I had been given box tickets to the circus at Madison Square Garden. We went, and my daughter brought a friend. The boxes resemble motel rooms and are equipped with a kitchenette completely stocked with every kind of drink imaginable. She had invited a new friend and was anxious to impress her by showing off. My thirteen-year-old wanted beer. I knew she would only sip the beer slightly because she didn't really like it, but I didn't know the other girl and how her parents felt about alcohol. Not wanting to embarrass my daughter and knowing that the girls were still children at heart, I allowed them to have some beer—but poured it over ice cubes. As I suspected, the beer went undrunk, but the ice cubes were sucked with fervor.

How your daughter handles alcohol will depend greatly on how she feels about herself in general and whether or not she has the courage to resist peer pressure. The teenager's excuse for drunkenness—that the world is such a lousy place and that they have so many pressures—is nothing more than an attempt to excuse weak behavior.

If your daughter is vulnerable in this area, don't condemn her or even punish her. Help her instead by directing her to appropriate counseling or clinics.

SUICIDE

Teens attempt suicide because they feel unloved or unworthy. They feel pressures they cannot cope with—from school, for social acceptance, from their parents, or from real or imagined deficiencies in themselves. Teens often don't realize the finality of suicide. They think they will be able to step outside of themselves and see how sorry their parents will be when they are gone.

If your daughter has attempted suicide, be grateful that her attempt failed. Don't be embarrassed by it. Don't try to cover it up or pretend it didn't happen. Get help right away. She may not fail the next time.

Also get immediate help if your daughter threatens suicide and life does not seem to be going too well for her in general. Do not pooh-pooh her threats and ignore her despondency as typical teenage behavior. Threatening to kill oneself if one doesn't get tickets to the next Rolling Stones concert is not the same as "If you don't let me go out Saturday, I'll kill myself . . . then you'll be sorry," or "If I wasn't around, you wouldn't have so much to worry about." If these are isolated statements and everything else—grades, friends, openness—is relatively normal, you can probably ignore them. However, if not, or if her words linger in your mind, get help. You are right in sensing danger.

RUNNING AWAY FROM HOME

One day you come home from work or shopping and find a note from your daughter that she has left home. Assuming that your daughter has not run away because she was beaten, starved or molested at home, she has probably run away because she feels unloved or unworthy of your love. Whatever the reason, immediately make all efforts to locate her. Any delay will merely reaffirm her feelings of inferiority.

If you locate her and she doesn't want to return, let her know that she will be welcome whenever she is ready. Find out what her plans are. Perhaps arrangements can be made for her to spend some time with relatives or friends until she feels she is ready to come back. Discuss the situation with your minister or others who know your daughter to see what else you should do at this time. Let her know how much you love her. Promise you will cooperate with her to help resolve whatever is troubling her . . . even if it is your behavior that is causing the problem.

Make good on your promises when she comes home. One teenage girl I know ran away from home because her parents were always criticizing her. The girl was well behaved and intelligent but very radical. The parents were always harping about her purple hair and her pacifist views. When the parents received word from the police that she was located, they immediately set out to bring her home. The girl was sensible enough to return with them, because she knew her alternative as a high-school dropout would mean fast-food employment forever. She tried to explain to her parents that she ran away because they didn't love who she was, that they were more concerned about how her looks and feelings reflected on them. Unfortunately, the parents never made any effort to change or to understand their daughter. The girl did not run away again—she just left home permanently when she became of age. The parents never heard from her. If only they had tried to accept their daughter, a lot of heartache could have been avoided.

Your daughter's running away is a signal that something is not right. When she returns home, make the effort to discover what that is and be flexible enough to modify your behavior and attitudes. You might want to consider discussing the situation with your minister or another third party. However, if your daughter wants to keep it a private matter and you feel the family can work out the difficulties, respect her wishes.

CULTS

If your daughter becomes involved with an extremist cult or a religion that requires complete separation from family and the values of our society, seek professional guidance. Your daughter may be having difficulty finding her own answers and is too readily accepting of the easy answers of others. She may be fearful that she doesn't have what it takes to make it in the real world. Since the leaders of these groups play for keeps, don't pass off your daughter's intentions as a passing fancy. If she is tempted by these groups, it is likely that she will not have the strength to pull away later even if she wants to. She needs immediate assistance to learn she has a right to control her own life and to be taught how to do it.

HITCHHIKING

You cannot warn your daughter enough about the dangers of hitchhiking. Set an example yourself by not hitchhiking or picking up hitchhikers. I know it is tempting to pick up a young female looking to hitch a ride because you are concerned about who else might pick her up. However, don't. If you pick up a hitchhiker who looks safe, your daughter may hitch a ride with someone *she* thinks looks safe.

Avoid temptation for your daughter by letting her know you will pick her up anywhere, anytime. Also, allow her some privacy. If, for example, she told you she was going to a party at Jenny's and she calls you from Lloyd's Bar to pick her up, don't question too deeply as to why she is not at Jenny's. Obviously she and her friends were out for some mischief. However, your wrath or punishment for deceiving you should not be so great that your daughter would rather risk a ride with a stranger than face you should a similar situation arise again.

SMOKING

You have just found out your daughter is a habitual smoker. You feel terrible. Unfortunately, there is not much else you can do. Smoking is an addiction which is very difficult to break, as many adults can attest to. Do not expect her to be a superior person and have greater willpower than most adults, or even yourself.

Don't waste your breath with threats of punishment. What you can do is reiterate in no uncertain terms the long-term hazards of smoking. Tell her how unattractive she will be because of bad breath and stained teeth. Make sure she is aware that smoking will reduce her chances of making the varsity team. Remind her that the money she spends on cigarettes would pay for that cross-country bike trip she is so eager to take next summer. Of course, if you or her father smokes, such a lecture will carry less weight.

Accept the fact that she is a smoker and help her to stop if she expresses any desire to do so. Perhaps you can encourage her to go to a stop-smoking clinic (along with you or her father if either of you smokes). She, however, should pay for her stop-smoking classes. If she starts and does not finish, she will not be able to say she never wanted to stop—that it was your idea. Smoking is her problem and she has to solve it.

If your daughter smokes, don't buy cigarettes for her or let her smoke in the house. She has no right to pollute your air. Use the tactics that many children use against their parents who smoke. The most timid children have been known to refuse to run to the store to buy cigarettes for their parents and to writhe on the floor in mock death whenever their parents light up, even if company is present. I wouldn't be surprised if today there are more adults than adolescents retreating to the bathroom for a smoke.

OTHER TOUGHIES

A DEATH IN THE FAMILY

While it's not uncommon for a grandparent to die during your daughter's teens, the effect on her will vary. It will depend partly on her relationship with the deceased. However, the most important element of how she reacts to the death will be her stage of emotional development at the time. If the death occurs during her intensely self-interested phase, she will exhibit very little emotion. Her attitude could probably be described as one of total unconcern. You can't believe it's the same girl who, six months ago, cried for days because her cat died. Don't be angry with her. Right now she's just not aware of anything but herself. It's a short phase but very intense. Just ignore it and keep her out of sight when the other relatives arrive. She is probably even too self-centered to be considerate of their feelings.

If your daughter shows no feeling and is not in her self-centered phase, have some patience. She may have a delayed reaction in a few weeks. This type of behavior is more likely to occur if the deceased was a parent, a brother or sister, or a close friend or grandparent. She may be feeling too great a loss for her to handle, or she may be harboring childish anxieties that she caused the death. It is important for her to face her emotions. Otherwise, she will grow up to be a fearful adult. If she still appears to have blocked out the death or refuses to deal with it and you cannot get her to open up, seek professional advice. Remember, though, your daughter may not be expressing feelings of sadness simply because she doesn't care. The person may not have been close to her or she may not see what all the fuss is about: "Aren't old people *supposed* to die?" If she feels this way but is considerate of your feelings, she's not really as hardhearted as she appears.

If your daughter doesn't want to go to a funeral or pay a condolence call, don't force her. Look at the situation from her point of view. For example, if your friend's mother died, there is no reason for her to attend if she doesn't want to. Consider her relationship with the deceased. A funeral or a condolence call is not

129

the place to show your daughter off or to puff up your own ego by displaying your ''obedient'' daughter to your friends and relatives. After all, it is unlikely that you would force your teenage son to accompany you in similar circumstances. Of course, you have every right to expect your daughter to cancel her plans in order to take care of younger siblings so you can attend the funeral or make the call. If, however, she's fearful of going to a funeral for someone close to her, explain that funerals are necessary because they help the survivors accept the finality of a loved one's demise. Explain that the funeral may be exceedingly painful, but it will make the loss easier to bear in the future. She probably does not want to go because she wants to keep the person alive in her mind. If you cannot convince her to attend, see that someone stays home with her. If she continues to have difficulty accepting the death, get professional advice.

DIVORCE

Divorce doesn't result in a broken home, only a broken marriage. Make sure your daughter understands that the marriage is the only relationship that is severed. Her home is still intact, as is her relationship with her father. All divorce means is that a husband and wife have decided to live separate lives with respect to their personal needs. Explain that she will have two homes instead of one.

There may be many adjustments with respect to the family life-style because of limited finances. You may need to work outside the home for the first time. Obviously, this will put you under a lot of pressure. Your daughter will be under more pressure too, as she may need to take on additional responsibilities. This is not the time for coq au vin, but if your daughter has already volunteered you to choreograph the Sophomore Sing, you will need to draw on whatever extra energy reserves you have. However, don't continue to try to be a supermom. In the future, you and she should remember that ''no'' is also an answer and be careful when you choose to do those things that will need extra effort.

There will also be adjustments as to the amount of time your daughter spends with her father. She should not feel pushed to spend more time with her father than before just because you and he choose to live apart. Let them work out their time together. It seems that where teen girls are involved, the most they have time for is a once-a-week dinner. Occasionally they can be lured away from their friends for a fishing trip or baseball game, but the usual female teenage activities of boy watching or shopping win out. Hopefully, her father will be understanding and will not feel rejected. It would be a good idea for him to invite your daughter's friends along occasionally. Often your daughter's friends' divorced fathers and their families become an extended family for your own daughter. This is a good substitute for the numerous aunts, uncles and cousins that used to live nearby before we became a mobile society.

Don't question your daughter about her time with her father except in general terms. Don't pump her for information or point out that he never spent $20 on dinner for *you*. However, you needn't be a saint. If he's late with the child support, you don't need to make excuses. After all, he is entitled to be accepted for who and what he is, just as you and your daughter are. Remember, though, that the relationship between your daughter and her father is crucial to her development. Encourage it!

SECOND MARRIAGE

Your daughter may have some difficulty accepting your second marriage. She may have secretly harbored the hope that you and her father would get back together again; she may be angry with you for being attracted to another man; she may be jealous of your second husband's place in your life; she may even feel disloyal to her natural father if she likes her stepfather.

You can allay your daughter's fears and bewilderment by letting her get to know your fiancé before the marriage. Let your daughter know that your new husband will not displace her—that you will still have time to give her all the love and attention she needs. You and her natural father should let your daughter know that her place in your hearts and minds will not change. Her natural father could assure your daughter that she's not disloyal to him because she likes her stepfather-to-be. He could explain that he doesn't see your fiancé as a rival, only as another person who will grow to love and care about her.

Involve your daughter in your wedding plans as much as possible. Take her with you if you're looking for a new home or an apartment, or at least let her see it before moving day. Let her help in any redecorating. She may especially want a particular piece of furniture or a grouping to stay as is, and you should try to disrupt her life as little as possible. If you ask for her assistance and she refuses or acts as if she doesn't care, don't push her. You've met her more than halfway. Besides, she may be secure enough about you and her natural father that she really doesn't care. But remember, anything she doesn't know about beforehand will be fuel for her fears that she will be left out of your life after the marriage, or used as an excuse not to like her stepfather. Also, if you are redecorating so as to accommodate another adult, don't exclude her room. You don't want her to feel like a second-class citizen in her own home. Perhaps this might be a good time to let her have her own phone line. You have to tread carefully here, though—you don't want her to think you are trying to bribe her.

When you have remarried, make sure that your daughter's life continues as before. Her friends should still be able to come for dinner or sleepovers. She should still be able to practice the tuba in the living room if that's where she normally practices. Remember, she has some tough adjustments to make. She needs to adjust to not being able to barge in on you whenever she feels like it; she may feel the need to wear a bathrobe for the first time in her life; she needs to adjust to having less of your undivided attention. Asking your new husband to adjust to the normal noise and clutter of a teen is only fair.

PHYSICAL ABUSE

If your daughter is repeatedly physically abusive to you or to others, seek professional help. Don't be embarrassed. Your daughter needs professional help to learn how to express herself through socially acceptable behavior. Even if you are the only one she is abusive to, seek help. You have a right not to be abused, and you and your daughter have a right to a positive relationship. Do not automatically feel her behavior is your fault. You don't get the credit for her accomplishments; she does. Therefore, you need not take the blame for her faults.

If you find yourself singling out your teenage daughter for physical or verbal abuse, get help for yourself immediately. Don't be too ashamed to admit the problem. The problem is not shameful. What is shameful is pretending it does not exist, or acknowledging its existence and not taking any action.

Don't hesitate. You owe it to your daughter and yourself to act before any abusive behavior becomes a police matter.

DISHONESTY

STEALING. Teenagers steal either because they are pressured into it by their peers or because they enjoy the thrill of it. If your daughter is caught stealing, don't make a federal case out of it and treat her as if she committed murder. Show your disappointment. Also show your love and concern by making it clear to her that you will help her, not by forgiving and forgetting but by recognizing that she may have a problem and by taking the appropriate action.

For example, if your daughter claims to have stolen because that's what her friends do, try to determine why she needs the acceptance of others who behave so differently from the way she was taught to behave. She may have too much pressure in her life and need some assistance coping with it. Perhaps she is being picked on too much at home or at school or her brother or sister completely outshines her. Be firm, but loving. Explain that she made a mistake which you do not expect her to repeat. See that she returns the items or pays for them and for any damage caused by the theft. Find out what she thinks would help her not to be vulnerable to peer pressure in the future. She may need some professional counseling. Be aware too that the peer group may be vengeful and a change of school or neighborhood may be needed.

It is a different problem if your daughter steals for excitement. That's a high, like a drug high, and her stealing should be treated as if it were an addiction. There will have to be a major change in your daughter's life-style so she will be able to channel her need for adventure into a more productive activity—or at least one that is not illegal. Looking at stealing objectively, it requires creative planning and generates a high level of exciting anticipation. She will either have to be directed toward not needing this excitement on a physical level, similar to drug withdrawal, or her needs will have to be rechanneled. You might be able to help her redirect her efforts (acting? hang-gliding? kyacking?) but will probably need outside help if ''withdrawal'' is the more feasible route, or if you get no cooperation from your daughter about redirecting her energies and talents.

If your daughter claims that this was her first theft and she will never do it again, believe her. She may just have wanted to see what it was like to do something wrong. Quite likely, her fear following her crime and being caught will act to prevent her from stealing again, simply because the experience was unpleasant. Your daughter is no different from most people, and people tend not to repeat behavior which had distasteful consequences. If the situation happens again, take the action described above.

Don't expect your daughter to be a saint. If you constantly leave your purse open or quarters for the washing machine lying around, expect to lose some money. Either she or her friend will dip in once in a while. However, if you allow this to happen often, your daughter will think you a fool and lose respect for you. Nobody really enjoys getting away with something—they feel cheated. If you suspect your daughter ''dips,'' don't waste your breath by confronting her. She will merely deny it. Just don't leave loose change around. She'll get the message and feel relieved. It's similar to not leaving knickknacks within reach of a two-year-old. The money jar can discreetly reappear at a later time, in a different location and in a different container, when your daughter's compulsion is directed toward something else—like boys or the telephone.

LYING. Children lie all the time. They will never own up to having finished the pie or bought another record. It's always you who must have finished the pie or a friend who loaned them the record. The tough part is not telling your daughter not to lie, but deciding how to answer when she asks you whether or not she should. Remember, if she's asking, she knows not to lie. She doesn't want to hear that she should never lie; she is asking for your advice. For example, my twelve-year-old daughter, who pays for her own movies, wanted to know if she should lie and say she was eleven so she could still pay the children's price. She wasn't asking what was the "right" thing to do. She already knew that she should pay full price. She was really asking for my permission to lie. I told her that as a parent I couldn't tell her to lie, but that I understood she didn't want to pay $5 for a movie instead of $2. I also agreed with her that people shouldn't pay adult prices unless they received adult privileges. We decided to pass the buck. She would hand a $5 bill to the cashier and say, "One, please." If she got change, fine. If not, *c'est la vie*.

Our solution may seem like a cop-out. However, my daughter learned that not all problems can be answered with a simple yes or no. Five dollars is a lot of money for a twelve-year-old to pay to see a movie. Often it is an entire week's allowance. Learning when to stretch rules is important. True, society cannot exist with everyone making his or her own rules, but neither can it exist with everybody following blindly. The former will result in anarchy and the latter in death from stagnation. You need not be afraid to let your daughter know of your rule bending. I'm sure most of us have bought an unaccompanied teen a movie ticket. Presumably their parents knew they were at the theater. This is not the same as buying a fourteen-year-old a six-pack of beer—a fourteen-year-old who is drunk may harm not only himself but others. Take care to let your daughter know your reasons when you deviate from the straight and narrow. Remember, there's a lot of gray area about lying and cheating. What kind of example do you set? When you buy airline tickets do you say your daughter is under twelve when she's fourteen? If you get the wrong change, do you return it? If someone in front of you drops a bill and you rush to pick it up with the intent of returning it, will you keep it if you discover it's a $20 bill instead of a $1 bill? These are tough questions for many adults and while most of us are honest, we may have had a bad day and keep that $20. Realistically, very few of us are 100 percent honest 100 percent of the time.

Your daughter is perceptive enough to realize this and will find your all-or-nothing answers to her questions about honesty inadequate. The best course to take is to answer her according to your own values. For example, I would not lie about my daughter's age for a few dollars, mainly because she would feel insulted. I have thought, though, that if the occasion arose, I would "stretch" the truth about a major item like a plane ticket— if she would let me get away with it. Also, I have no hesitation about lying about my daughter's age with respect to having her accompany me to certain places where minors are not allowed. However, whenever I bend the rules, I explain my reasons to my daughter. I want her to know that at certain times she might feel the need to break a rule and that it should not be done lightly. Sometimes we have to "walk" when the sign says "don't walk." We are humans, not sheep, and as a result we think and feel. I do not want my daughter growing up and blindly obeying every rule. I want her to feel free and be free to question. However, if and when she breaks a rule, she should have good reason to and be aware of the consequences.

CHEATING. Your daughter comes home furious. It seems everybody cheated on a chemistry exam which she had studied hard for. Don't ask whether or not she cheated too. If she didn't, she will tell you; if she did, your asking would only cause her to lie. It is much better to listen first to all she has to say about the incident. You will soon be able to discern whether or not she participated in any wrongdoing. When she has had her say, point out, of course, that people who cheat on exams really cheat themselves. If you believe she acted with integrity during the exam, your tone should be one of empathy. Explain that you understand how she feels, especially after putting so much time and energy into preparing for the exam. This is not the time for a lecture about cheating. She didn't cheat, so she's not in need of a lecture. What she needs is notice and affirmation of her exemplary behavior.

If you suspect her of cheating, do not react as if she committed murder. Cheating is certainly wrong, but the person harmed most by her act is herself. Try to find out why she cheated by asking if she has any idea why her friends cheated. Perhaps it was to be part of the crowd, or perhaps the exam was unusually difficult. Perhaps the students were under pressure from their families to get an A. You will get some kind of response from her and you should proceed accordingly. For example, if she says the children are all under pressure to get A's because they all want to go to Harvard, explain that one test mark is not going to make a difference. You might also consider whether or not you expect too much of your daughter. Perhaps she cheated because she was afraid of failing and was too embarrassed to let you know she needs a tutor.

The most worrisome reason for her cheating, or for her letting someone copy her paper, would have been if she had done so because of peer pressure. If you suspect this as the reason, but she is not usually susceptible to peer pressure, reiterate your "cheating is wrong" lecture as strongly as possible. However, if she seems to go along with the crowd most of the time, try to find out why she is so insecure. Perhaps she is given too much freedom, or not enough, and is unsure of your feelings about her. Perhaps she is unhappy with her looks, and a classy haircut or a visit to a dermatologist may give her a needed lift.

If you cannot find out what is causing her insecurity or cannot help her to become more confident, seek professional assistance before her vulnerability to peer pressure involves her in something more serious.

PEER PRESSURE

If your daughter has her own values, she should be able to withstand peer pressure. If you have never used what others do as an excuse for your own behavior, your daughter probably won't either. If you cheat on your income tax because "everyone does it," do not be surprised to learn that your daughter cheats on exams for the same reason. Most peer pressure, however, is trivial and you should be amused by it. There's no need for you to bring out the big guns when your daughter gets one ear pierced because "everyone" is doing it. It's natural for her to want to *look* like her friends, but that's not the same as *being* like them. Both of you should be aware of the difference.

Also, remember it's fun to squeal in a crowd as a teeny-bopper. What you want is that your daughter be part of the group but have the backbone to leave the crowd when it goes against her beliefs. If she cannot, she needs help, not just your admonitions. Find alternatives to her peer group. If you are unable to do so, get outside advice.

LEAVING THE NEST

Sometimes teens leave home right after high school. They marry, or get their own apartments or declare themselves financially independent while at college. If your daughter has left the nest, whether or not you agree with her life-style, you cannot treat her the same as you would a daughter living at home. You can ask that your daughter living at home call to say she will be late, but you cannot expect your independent daughter to keep you apprised of her comings and goings, even though she may be only seventeen. When she does call or visit, don't complain that she is not giving you enough attention. Let her know how much you appreciate hearing from or seeing her. If you don't hassle her, she will let you in on more of her life.

Don't fault her for repeating your life even if you have often expressed how sorry you were that you married so early or did not finish college. Don't feel you've failed. How she lives is her choice. If she and her boy friend decide to live together, don't disown her even if you disapprove. You need not condone it, either, by being pushed into extending weekend invitations to them to stay in your daughter's bedroom. What you need to do is accept her decision and let her know that you will be around when and if she needs you. Remind her, though, that while you have adjusted to her living with her boy friend, Thanksgiving dinner, with all the relatives gathered, is not the time or place for her to make the announcement.

Also, don't be too ready to help your independent married daughter.* Remember, help does not mean being at her beck and call or always doing what she asks. If, for example, your daughter and her spouse do not know how to manage money and always come to you for help, it need not be a handout. You might be helping them more by not giving them additional money and directing them to a budget counselor. Of course, helping out in a real emergency is a different matter, but the mortgage being due

* But see Pregnancy, page 114.

138

or the car breaking down is not an emergency; they are foreseeable events.

Consider your financially dependent college or working daughter as having left the nest also, even if she still lives at home. You may still have the right to know when she will be home—but just as a courtesy to you. However, your daughter is a young woman now and should be treated as such. If she's working and living at home, she should contribute part of her salary for household expenses. She should have and pay for her own telephone. She should not need any money from you except perhaps for a car or a vacation if you are in a position to afford them. A dressy winter coat might be a welcome Christmas gift for your working-girl daughter. She's probably living at home to save money for her own apartment or for an upcoming marriage. If the former, don't make it so cozy for her that she will never want to leave or make her feel guilty when she does. Our society expects adults to live on their own, and she should want to be on her own as soon as she is financially able.

Whether she's working or attending college, she shouldn't be expected to be at home to eat with the family most of the time. You needn't prepare a special dinner for her. If she's not home at mealtime, she is perfectly capable of fixing her own dinner. Don't nag that you have prepared her favorite food and she's never home to eat it. Conversely, she shouldn't complain to you that there's "nothing to eat" in the house.

As an adult, she should be expected to be considerate of other family members. She no longer occupies a privileged position where any inconsiderate behavior can be passed off as a stage she's going through. Explain to her she can't have it both ways. It will be difficult for both of you at first—you will be called on to alternate between being a mother (upon news of academic probation) and a friend (she will invite you out to dinner, her treat).

8
EVERYDAY CRISES

ILLNESS

FAMILY. It is hard on a family when illness strikes. Even if the prognosis is good or the illness temporary, the entire family is under extra strain. As a mother, you are the one who is responsible for any reorganization that is necessary. This is often true even if you are the one who is ill!

Some children react well under stress; others nearly fall apart. When anyone is ill, conserve your energy for what needs to be done at the time, and worry about exhibitions of selfishness on your daughter's part later. However, you must realize that no matter how ill your husband or another child may be, your teen daughter has needs of her own at this time.

Your husband may be scheduled for an operation the same day your daughter makes her debut as pitcher for the local softball team. Just because your neighbors think that you should be at your husband's side doesn't mean you should be. What does your husband think? Maybe he will feel worse if he knows you are not at the game rooting for his daughter. How important is it to her that you be there? While community customs should be considered, don't let them dictate your decision.

It is normal for your daughter to feel resentful and deprived of attention if, for example, illness requires you to be at another child's side day and night. She may understand that you need to be there, but understanding doesn't make her feel better. Try to explain to her that there will be times when she will come first and it need not necessarily have anything to do with illness. Remind her of the time she starred in the school play and you took over her chores for two months so she could spend her time rehearsing, or the time the whole family was put out of the living room for a week because she needed the space to conduct an experiment. If your daughter is very intense about her needs, follow the advice under Selfishness on page 36.

HERS. Your daughter may be one of those lucky ones who never even get a cold. However, if she is the type that catches everything that's going around at least twice, you need a lot of patience and self-control. You need not stay home with your daughter unless she's very ill, but remember, everyone wants extra attention when they are sick. If you can't stay home, leave a tray set for her lunch. Fix up a pretty fruit plate for her. Call home, especially in the afternoon when illness usually peaks.

Some teens will use an illness as an excuse to stay home from school as much as possible; others will go even when they're sick. The thought of being parted from their friends for even a day is too much for them. Absent any excessive excuses, let your daughter decide whether or not to stay home. After all, no one else knows how she feels. In our house, if my daughter is undecided, the policy is to take a shower and have a light breakfast. Usually, if she can face the toast, she will opt for school. My daughter always gets angry with me because I don't tell her to stay home. What she wants is a day off without guilt. I always tell her she can stay home if she wants to, but I will not give her a "mental health" day. My feeling is that school to her is just like my job to me. There are days when I feel lousy and I go anyway, just as there are days when I feel physically fine but need a day to catch up or do nothing but loaf. Your daughter is entitled to an occasional "mental health" day, too, but she should be the one to decide when she needs it.

If your daughter is sick often and there is no medical reason for it, she is probably just highly susceptible to viruses. I know you try to make sure she takes vitamins, eats a proper diet, gets enough rest and does plenty of exercise. However, even with your efforts and hers, she still gets sick. She'll probably outgrow her susceptibility.

In the meantime, don't try to nag your daughter back to health. She has to learn that if she is susceptible she needs to take care of herself. She shouldn't stay home if it is raining, only take an umbrella. It doesn't mean that she must come home at 10:00 p.m. on a Saturday night, but it does mean that she shouldn't have been out late the night before, worked all day Saturday and then stay out late Saturday night. Don't try to keep her in—she'll still catch things from her classmates anyway. If you both do the best you can and she still gets sick (and she probably will), help her accept it with good humor. Don't say, ''See, I told you it was too cold to go to the beach.'' She feels bad enough about missing her class picnic or having to cancel two babysitting jobs. She'll outgrow her susceptibility, but don't let it destroy your relationship in the meantime.

If serious illness strikes your teenage daughter, your biggest concern, after knowing she will recover, is how she feels about herself. For example, many teens suffer long bouts with mononucleosis and as a result may miss a summer or drop back in school. Their question is ''Why me? I planned to have such a good time this summer.'' If you are religious, your faith helps with the answer. If you are not religious, find some way to turn the discomforts of illness into a positive experience. When I was faced with that question, I responded, ''I don't know . . . but I do know you will get better and that sometime in your life, knowing you had suffered and survived will help you out in a difficult situation.'' Don't point out how much better off than others she is— she will counter with how much better off others are than she.

Instead, empathize with her about missing out on a summer of fun. Let her know you agree that it's rotten luck. Talk about the future—the clothes she plans to buy for the fall or the colleges she would like to apply to. Don't make her feel guilty or let her worry about the hospital or doctor bills. Remind her that you've saved for a rainy day and the rainy day is here—and you're well prepared for it.

You must also remember that when your daughter is sick, no one is supposed to have a good time. My daughter's friend, who had a rather serious operation, told me that she was annoyed at her mother because her mother laughed sometimes when she visited her at the hospital. My own daughter showed similar behavior when she returned home from the hospital. Whenever she heard anyone laughing, I would hear this little voice, "M-o-m-m-y." Poor thing, the world went on while she was sick. Be gentle. It is very tempting to tell her off when she is so demanding, but she *is* sick. It is normal for her to feel left out and want some extra attention. Keep a sense of humor and don't let her demands get to you. Naturally, if they continue beyond a reasonable point, you will need to handle the situation as you would a two-year-old who always asks for water at night. Good luck!

RELIGION

Sometime during her teens, your daughter will go through a religious phase. She will be very intense about her feelings and beliefs. She may speak of joining a religious order. Other teens may embrace philosophy with the fervor of the most devout. They become apostles of Thoreau or Kahlil Gibran. Some may decide the Eastern religions are their path to self-awareness. Others become cultish about being a vegetarian or believing in reincarnation. At the other extreme are those who become devout atheists, declaring all those who believe in any religion to be fools. As with most things your daughter espouses as a teen, it's best to pay as little attention to her pronouncements as possible. Don't tell her she's foolish or doesn't know what she's talking about. She knows how you feel and what you believe. She's just exploring new ideas. Let her find her own way.*

If you are a religious person, do not force your daughter to attend services if she doesn't want to. Conversely, you should honor your daughter's desire to be confirmed even if you are not religious yourself. You want your daughter to develop inner strength. She can develop it by believing in herself. She takes her beliefs seriously and so should you. You must let your daughter feel she is her own person and has control over her own life. She's the one who has to make decisions about drugs and sex

*But see Cults, p. 127.

when she's with her peers. If you make her feel that her inner beliefs are silly or wrong, she will not have the inner security to do what she feels is right. That doesn't mean you should change what you believe. Just allow her the right to believe what she wants. Furthermore, her religious fervor or lack of any is probably temporary, and if you are supportive of her, she will end up believing pretty much as you do.

If your daughter balks at continuing her religious training or attending services after she has been confirmed, don't react as if she is rejecting her faith completely. More likely, it is a statement that from then on she is going to do what she believes. Just express your disappointment and your hope that she will resume attending on a regular basis, without making a major issue of it. It will be easier for her to return if she doesn't need to worry about losing face. She's not going to forget all she's been taught. She just wants to let you know that from now on she's going to act on her own ideas. Don't be surprised to discover that she believes as you do—only don't tell her that!

KEEPING THINGS FROM HER

Don't be afraid to let your daughter know about the dark side of life. Whether it's a death or serious illness in the family or the loss of a job, don't hide the situation. There are unpleasant aspects of life that we all have to deal with in one way or another. Things may happen to us or to our friends. You and your daughter should deal with them in perspective and, where possible, have a sense of humor.

For example, a friend was recently fired from a job the day before her daughter was scheduled to take a scholarship exam. My friend planned not to tell her daughter about the new calamity until after the exam. However, she wound up telling her that same night because a good opportunity arose. Her daughter was to be a counselor at sleep-away camp and had to make her own transportation arrangements to get there. Originally, my friend was going to take a vacation day from work and drive her there. However, the evening she got fired, her daughter told her she would go by public bus because she didn't want her mother to take the time. It was the perfect opportunity. My friend responded, "Honey, I've got plenty of time—I just got fired. Do you want to go Wednesday? Thursday? Friday?" They had a good laugh together.

My friend presented something fairly ominous in a favorable way. The loss of a job would mean more time with the family, for a little while at least. Some good can be found in almost anything. Death often means the end of suffering; divorce, the end of arguments.

There are, however, some truly tragic moments for which no adequate words or humor can be found—the death of a parent, a child or a special friend. Don't hide the news or try to cover your feelings so your daughter won't know. It's best just to let the grief flow and allow her to be a part of your grief, and to grieve herself. She has a right to feel bad if you do.

On the other hand, you may find your daughter disinterested or unaffected when you tell her of a tragedy or misfortune that has occurred in the family. Don't be angry with her or worry about her lack of feeling. This might just be a moment in her life when she is having real difficulty dealing with her own fears and cannot handle another calamity occurring outside her control.

HER ROOM

You may not be able to provide your daughter with her own room. On the other hand, some teen girls who have their own rooms never stay there. It is best to keep a flexible outlook about your daughter's attitude toward her room whether or not she shares it.

If it is her own room and she wants to be messy and resents your straightening it out, respect her wishes. However, if the Board of Health has sent a condemnation notice or the bugs have taken over, assert your rights. Otherwise, let her keep it her way, as it is her room. If she shares a room, though, she should keep it neat (or let you do it) out of respect for her brother or sister.

Sometimes very social children do not like to stay in their

rooms. For example, your daughter may have a desk, good lighting and lots of space in her room, but she does her homework in front of the television or at the kitchen table. She says she works better with noise around her. It is her homework and if she likes to do it that way, that should be fine with you. However, you may not like the mess in the kitchen or living room. Don't carry on about how much better it is for *her* to do her homework in her room. Rather, be honest and explain you don't like looking at her mess. The conflict between her need for company and your need for the uncluttered look might be resolved with her own television or stereo, or a phone extension in her room, or by limiting her living room space to the coffee table.

If your daughter shares a room and she is the older occupant, she considers it *her* room. The younger child accepts this and realizes that it is her* sister's room and that she is merely "allowed" to sleep there. This goes against adult sensibilities, but children respect territorial rights and the older one was there first. It is best not to interfere with what your children perceive to be the natural order. It is easier for you to get used to having the younger child practice the violin or do homework in the living room than it is to hear them squabbling all the time. Endless comments, threats or suggestions to the younger child that she go to her room are pointless, because she has no room to go to.

Constantly trying to have them share the room equally will only result in their being hostile toward each other. Your teen daughter will not share, and all you will have achieved is impressing upon the younger child that she is getting the short end of the stick. Your older daughter will never relinquish her "rights." It is better to work on the younger child to be as inconspicuous as possible when using the living room. Her time will come when your older daughter leaves home. (Of course, your older daughter will seethe about the younger child having her own room—*she* never did. If you point out that she had her own room before her sister was born, she will reply that it doesn't count—she was too young to appreciate it then.)

---

* I realize that siblings of different sexes often share a bedroom. The use of the feminine pronoun is used here merely for convenience.

SLEEPOVERS

By the time your daughter is a teenager, sleeping over at some-one's house shouldn't be a big deal. By now she and her friends should be responsible enough to get to sleep at a reasonable hour if the sleepover is on a school night. Even if they don't, one night without enough sleep won't cause your daughter any harm.

There's really no reason not to allow sleepovers, even on weekdays. It's good for your daughter to show off her manners and converse with other adults in a weekday atmosphere. Week-end sleepovers are usually after parties and involve breakfast when no one else is up or around except your daughter and her friend. Weekday sleepovers often result from a special school project or midweek school concert. This gives your daughter a chance to learn about another family and also to act responsibly and to be proud of herself. She will come home and tell you she washed the salad vegetables, put the baby to bed and won a game of chess. She will say they went to sleep at 11:00 p.m. and she remembered to make the bed in the morning. Don't deny your daughter an opportunity to feel proud of herself, or yourself the opportunity to be proud of her. Don't restrict her freedom unnecessarily.

Of course, if you have reason to believe that the other child or host family will behave in a way which is harmful to your daugh-ter, you have every right to veto the sleepover. Trust your instincts. If you do not give your daughter permission to sleep over, be honest with her as to the reasons why. (Note that your daughter may say she doesn't need your permission and just storm out. There's not much you can do then except chastise her for her manners and look closely at your relationship to see why she needs to openly defy you.) Most likely, she will respect your wishes but argue that you don't know what you're talking about. In that case, the old adage ''he doth protest too much'' will be a good indication of how on-target you are.

Remember, however, that often one child will be the one who sleeps out and one will be the child who sleeps in. I'm sure you wouldn't mind if your daughter always had her friends stay over, so you are probably safe in assuming that the host family doesn't mind your daughter practically "living in" either. These things tend to run in cycles, but your daughter may just like to go out all the time. Don't look at it as a rejection of her home. More likely, she feels so safe and secure that she's never afraid to leave it. If you feel odd, though, it's probably because you're worrying what the host family is thinking. Don't waste your time—they know you're not an ogre. Remember, they have a teenage daughter too. If you still feel funny, have your daughter take a bag of oranges or oatmeal cookies with her the next time she visits.

PRACTICING

Piano lessons, dance instruction, art classes all cost a lot of money these days. You want to be sure your daughter is getting your money's worth. So you push her to practice, practice, practice. However, if you constantly need to push and prod your daughter to practice and there is no progress, there is no point in continuing if it is causing unnecessary friction between you. By the time your daughter reaches her teens you will both know where her ambitions lie. Remember, it is ambition, not talent alone, that gets the budding actress more than a few bit parts, or the figure skater to the Olympics, but ambition is not a trait that can be pushed. It can be squashed, or nourished and encouraged, but not forced. If your daughter is a talented violinist but is satisfied only to be playing in the high-school orchestra, you cannot force her to try for Carnegie Hall. (On the other hand, be careful not to squash your daughter's ambition even if you feel she has no talent. That is for her to find out, not for you to tell her. Of course it is natural for you to want to protect her feelings, but she has to learn her own limitations for herself. Besides, sometimes great ambition compensates for very little talent.)

There are many stories about children who succeeded because they were pushed by their parents. My guess is that the "pushed" children were just as ambitious as their parents, but just not as aggressive. They let someone do the pushing for them, but underneath they themselves had a great ambition to succeed. It is irrelevant whether their ambition was based on an overwhelming desire to be somebody or to please their parents. Let your daughter continue the lessons even if she doesn't practice, if it's no financial strain and she enjoys them. It's not necessary for you to push her to practice and run the risk of hurting your relationship or spoiling something that she simply enjoys. If she wants to stop the lessons, let her, but don't feel that they were wasted. Any skill or talent she has developed will give her pleasure later on in life, even if she seems completely turned off to the activity now.

"BUT I WANT TO SEE YOUR SCHOOL PLAY!"

Adolescents can be real party-poopers. You've played Romeo to her Juliet all fall. You've gotten all your friends and co-workers to buy tickets for her school play. The flowers are ordered and your new dress is hanging in the closet, already hemmed. The big night is two days away and you're crying. Your daughter has just told you, "I didn't know you were planning to go. I don't want you to go to my play." Thinking she was concerned about her performance, you reassured her that she'd do fine, but then she flat out told you not to go, that she would be embarrassed if you were there.

You're crying partly because you are angry with her but mostly because it's not fair to you. You know other parents will be there. Why does your daughter always say she won't go with you? Why does she let other parents pick her up from school concerts or late parties, but not you? Why is it you can never be there to bask in her glory? You're right, it isn't fair. However, if you and your daughter get along reasonably well, don't make a big deal out of her not wanting you around. It isn't worth the time to second-guess her reasons. Let her know you would like to go and that you think she is being unfair. Realize, too, that you will probably not be wanted at camp visiting days or asked to go to college parent weekends.

Of course, some parents would be relieved never to have to sit through school band concerts or freeze at college football weekends. However, they have children who insist their parents attend every play, every concert, every camp or college function. Naturally, for those parents, there is always some sort of schedule conflict. The junior-high concert is on the same night as the senior-high play, or an important business meeting is sched-

149

uled for the night of her dance recital. Your daughter, the martyr, told you six months ago that it would be okay if you missed her recital—she "understands." Of course, she has told you that at least ten times a week for the past six months. Life is not fair!

BOY-CRAZY

It seems all your daughter and her friends talk and think about is boys. Muffled giggles sail through the house. The telephone rings incessantly, and often no one admits to being at the other end. It probably began after last Halloween when the neighborhood boys and girls ran down the streets or through the apartment-building hallways squirting each other with shaving cream.

During this stage of your daughter's development, there is more talk than action. Very little boy/girl association actually goes on, but because of her preoccupation you are worried that she will become boy-crazy. Relax . . . she is just behaving normally and taking a peek into her future. She's not ready to date yet, unless somebody pushes her. One young girl I know, who was invited on a date during a four-way telephone conversation, took her best friend along.

The big question today is whether or not it is proper for a girl to invite a boy out. It has always been proper for a girl to invite a boy to be her escort, or to come to her home to listen to records. Personally, I think if a girl invites a boy out, she should pay. Also, I don't think it is appropriate for a girl to call a boy to find out why he hasn't called her. Let your daughter know how you feel about the subject and why. However, she has the right to handle the situation in a way that is comfortable for her. For example, if your daughter is an aggressive, take-charge person, it would be out of character for her to wait for the phone to ring. Besides, if she had to act at being demure, any relationship she had with a boy would not be an honest one. If she has an aggressive personality, she may have fewer boy friends, but at least the ones she will have will like *her*, not someone she pretends to be.

Don't make an issue out of your daughter calling or "chasing" a boy. Use common sense as your guide. She should be instructed that calls to anyone should be made at a reasonable hour and not during dinner time. Also, if she invites a boy to a particular outing and he refuses without suggesting an alternative, good manners dictate that she should not call that boy again and make a pest of herself. He may just not be ready to date yet.

Being a teenage girl and "discovering" boys should be fun. It shouldn't immediately bring an accusation of boy-craziness or an onslaught of lectures about contraception or promiscuity. Let her enjoy her silliness. I know two fourteen-year-old girls who paraded up and down a certain street hoping to "accidentally" run into certain neighborhood boys. Their excuse for being on that street was that they were out walking the dog. Of course, they were over a mile from home, and it was obvious that the dog, being no more than a young puppy, would have died from exhaustion had it actually walked (instead of being carried) that far. Such game playing is never truly outgrown. I know a recent college grad who, whenever she has a date for dinner, arranges for several friends to call so her date will think she is popular. Some male friends of mine often ask me to do the same for them when they are entertaining women.

Give your daughter a chance to know boys as people, not only as dates. Don't think she's boy-crazy if a lot of her friends are boys. We have learned that people from different cultures who get to know each other better get along better. It is likely that the better the different sexes understand and know each other, the better they too will get along.

DATING

There's no set age when your daughter should begin to date. If her first invitation comes when she is a young teen and she has not been pressured into dating, her reaction will probably be, "Why would I want to go to a movie with a boy?" This is a likely response from a thirteen-year-old who feels comfortable with herself and has not yet begun to menstruate. However, a thirteen-year-old who is physically mature may be ready to date.

Look for cues from your daughter before you take a position on dating. Remember, you don't need to take any position until she has been asked out. Find out whether your daughter *wants* to date. It may be she doesn't want to but thinks she should. Has the family been subtly teasing her into dating? Give your daughter the freedom to refuse until she is ready. Also, before you take a position on dating, consider your values and the customs of your community, as well as your daughter's needs. Be realistic. You may be able to keep your sixteen-year-old daughter from dating, but at what cost? You're fortunate if the sixteen-year-olds in your area don't date, but forbidding your daughter to date when all her friends do could cause an irreparable breach between the two of you. Perhaps you should reexamine your position and see if there is room for compromise.

Let your daughter find her own level and then use your judgment accordingly. Her biological clock may be quite different from what yours was at her age. It may also be quite different from her friends'. Even in the same apartment building, there may be girls who have gone steady since the age of fourteen and others who never had a date in high school. None are strange. They are just different. Make sure you don't push your daughter to date. For example, a certain boy kept calling my daughter and asking her out to the movies. She kept refusing and finally wouldn't come to the phone any more when he called. His father called me to find out what was wrong with his son. I explained that nothing was wrong with his son, only that my daughter was moving slowly socially. She wasn't ready to date. She had not even begun the telephone giggles about boys. She had just begun to shower on a daily basis. It turned out that the boy's friends all had girl friends and he felt he would be safe with my "neuter" daughter because he wasn't ready to date yet, either. I'm sure the boy felt relieved to know that there were other socially slow teens in the world. My daughter later learned to use her slow-developing sexuality to her advantage. When she started high school in ninth grade, she looked eleven years old. However, she found she was exceedingly popular. All the boys who hadn't begun to grow flocked to her because she looked "safe." She was able to develop friendships among the boys and learn how to get along with males on an equal, casual basis.

Other than knowing who the boy is and where he lives, don't insist on a full report. Don't treat every new suitor as a potential husband. Your daughter may feel shy, so don't embarrass her with too many questions. Of course, you should know where she is going and when she will be home. Besides, it is not unusual for parents to be kept in semi-darkness these days about their daughter's boy friends. A transient society and working parents have loosened neighborhood ties. Also, many young women go away to college where they meet and fall in love with young men from other parts of the country. One family I know was kept in the dark until Christmas break of her daughter's senior college year, when her daughter announced she was getting married after graduation. The family had only fleetingly heard of the young man and had never met him. Your first reaction is "What kind of parents are they that they had no idea their daughter was going with someone?" But think again. The parents didn't need to be told. They knew their daughter. Evidently, their daughter was given enough guidance to be able to finish college and want to marry and live a life like her parents'. The daughter knew her parents trusted her, and she knew they would accept her fiancé without question. Being kept informed of the status of your daughter's relationship with her boy friend may make you feel better, but it doesn't make the relationship better or worse, or the boy friend a more or less acceptable suitor.

There's no reason for you not to restrict dating to the weekends if you want to. You can explain that dating is fun—it's play time. The midweek is for work—whether a job, or housework or school work. Our society is geared for play on weekends. Weekends are our reward for a week's work well done. Explain that she will enjoy her dates more when she's not swinging in too many directions at once. It's hard to go from school girl to part-time waitress to student to daughter to femme fatale all in one evening. Remind her that if her life has a steady pace she will get sick less often, have more energy and be able to enjoy her weekend dates a lot more.

Going steady may be a must in your area or in your daughter's school, just as in some communities it's hard to live as a single adult. Going steady does prevent your daughter from learning about other boys. However, for some girls, it may be a type of freedom. Going steady may give your daughter security to freely pursue her studies or other interests. She doesn't have to spend time "cruising" or wondering whether or not she'll have a date for the Sophomore Hop. Intervene only if the relationship is

153

harmful to your daughter, not because you don't like the idea of her going steady. See if the relationship is putting too much pressure on her sexually, or drawing her energy from other areas which are important to her. If it isn't, there is no reason for you to try to break it up.

If you do interfere with your daughter's going steady, or prohibit her from dating a certain boy without reasonable grounds, you run the risk of forcing her to sneak out. There should not be any reason for your daughter to date anyone on the sly. If you do not approve of the boy and your disapproval has a reasonable basis, certainly voice your feelings loudly and clearly, but don't forbid her unless you actually fear for her physical safety. It is better for her to go against your wishes openly. This way, at least you know where she is. She will think twice anyway about what you've said. Remember, if she is on a sneak date, she may be afraid to call you if she's in trouble. Also, it is likely that you will discover her sneakiness and then you will be mistrustful of her. If she sneaks out and loses your trust, she is well on the way to not liking herself. If you trust her to make her own judgments about people, it is likely that soon she will come to the same conclusions as you.

"WHERE ARE YOU GOING?"

Teens today do not make plans—everything is decided at the last possible moment. I am sure there must be some societal reason for this; perhaps the underlying threat of the here today, gone tomorrow nuclear syndrome, or the fluctuating interest rates, but whatever the reason, the result is the same. You are hereby forewarned that your daughter will receive an 8:00 p.m. telephone call to go to a 9:00 p.m. party which she will swear that neither she nor her friends knew anything about before. If you persist in your questions, you will probably be told that the teen who is to host the party didn't know about it before either.

We, of course, were brought up not to run out at the last minute. I never understood why I was not allowed to do that, so when the situation arose with my daughter, I was unconvincing in my argument that she not go. I had no answer when she asked,

"Why not?" I was, however, able to maintain certain other parental rights, but only with a great deal of negotiation. The scenario was as follows.

Setting: 8:00 p.m., Friday evening.

SHE: (After hanging up phone.) I'm going to wash my hair.
ME: So late, dear?
(Daughter already in shower.)
SHE: (After blow-drying hair.) Beth and I are going to a party.
ME: Now? Tonight? At the last minute? I don't want you to go. You shouldn't run out any time someone calls you.
SHE: Why not?
ME: It's just not nice—don't ask me why.
SHE: That's not a reason. What difference does it make if I was asked out at 6:00 p.m. or 8:00 p.m.?
ME: (Silence.) Where's the party?
SHE: I don't know.
ME: (Incredulous.) You don't know? How can you go to a party if you don't know where it is?
SHE: Beth knows. I'm meeting her in the lobby downstairs.
ME: Fine. When Beth comes, buzz up with the name and address of the party.
SHE: (Hesitantly.) She doesn't know either.
ME: (Astonished.) Wait a minute . . . how can you go to a party if neither of you knows where it is?
SHE: (With a how-could-you-be-so-stupid look.) We know *where* it is, we just don't know the address. It's the corner building on Maple and First.
ME: Well, whose party is it?
SHE: We don't know. We'll ask the doorman for the apartment number of the party.
ME: (Counting to ten, very slowly.) If the doorman tells you the apartment without your knowing even the name, it is certainly not the kind of party you belong at.
SHE: (With another how-could-you-be-so-stupid look.)

155

Mother! Don't you think Beth and I have enough sense to leave if it is *that* kind of party?

ME: (Not really too sure, but firmly.) You will have to call me and let me know the name and address as soon as you get there.

SHE: I won't . . . I'm not a baby.

ME: Honey, when the man on the news asks, "Do you know where your children are?" I need to be able to tell him. I need to be able to tell the police where you went when I send them out looking for your body in the morning.

SHE: (Disgusted sigh.) I *won't* call you from the apartment.

ME: I can't let you go out without knowing where you're going. I wouldn't be doing my job.

SHE: (Resigned to putting up with Mother.) There's a phone booth across the street from the building. When the doorman tells us the apartment, I will call you with the name and address.

Epilogue: 9:20 p.m. Telephone rings. "Hi, Ma? The doorman wouldn't tell us the apartment. We're going to the school dance instead. It's just a block from here. I'll be home by midnight." (The dance was a dud and she was home before 11:00 p.m.)

If you want your daughter to stay home and she wants to go out, unless you have a reason for her to stay, allow her to go. Your reason could be as simple as that you would like her to stay to keep you company. Otherwise, it is like asking her to put on a sweater because you are cold. You should always know where she is going, with whom and when she will be home. If your daughter realizes that you need this information not to check up on her or because you don't trust her to make the right decision, but for her safety and your peace of mind, she will be honest with you. Teenagers, just like most adults, will rise to the responsibility given to them. If you treat your daughter mistrustfully or as if she were seven years old, she will fulfill your negative expectations. Give your daughter your care and your trust; she is not likely to misuse them.

156

SENIOR YEAR

All that your daughter has heard and read has led her to believe wonderful things will happen to her during her senior high-school year, but in reality it may be a big letdown. Tell her not to feel cheated if her life is not as described in the books. Explain that she is much luckier than her counterparts of a generation ago. She has so many more options available to her upon high-school graduation that her senior year need not be a splendid end in the guise of a splendid beginning.

Today, by the time they reach their senior year, many teen girls are simply too mature to still be in high school. Many turn eighteen before graduation. Yet while they can vote, marry, work and join the army without parental consent, they still need an absence note signed by a parent. Furthermore, today's teen girls are far more worldly than their counterparts of the past. They have traveled and been to summer camp. They have been exposed to culture as never before, thanks in part to modern communications technology and society's growing concern with the arts. Even the smallest towns have expanded their cultural facilities, so that what once was available only in large cities is now available in varying degrees almost everywhere. In many communities this awareness, combined with tightened public and personal funds, has reduced or eliminated traditional senior-year activities.

As a result, you are faced with a bored, mature teenager who is in a year-long holding pattern. You could point out that a generation or so ago, senior year marked the end of childhood, and high-school graduation, the commencement of adulthood. However, for the majority of teen girls, it was really the beginning of a routine job or the tediums attendant to an early marriage and child rearing. For many, senior year remained the high point of their lives. Often the football hero and prom queen never reached comparable heights as adults, and after being launched into adulthood with so much fanfare, they became bitter because of their disillusionment.

As a parent, though, you are angry because your heart aches for your daughter. She is so beautiful and full of life and so impatient to start on her chosen path. She's so eager to apply what she has already learned about life that it is difficult for her to simply attend high school and be told not to chew gum in class. In the past, senior-year activities gave life some meaning during this time, but now she just waits. She waits to hear from the college of her choice, she waits to see what her friends will do, she waits for the year to end. You fear that as an alternative to the status quo, she may become pregnant or run off or drop out of school. You fear that the impatience of youth will overpower her reason.

During this time be understanding and supportive. Encourage her to take an evening course at the local college or become active in community affairs at an adult level. This may help to alleviate some of her sense of loss. Explain that in the long run she will be the more fortunate. Society or her community may have cheated her out of a glorious senior year but that does not mean she has been cheated out of life. Explain that knowing she survived a difficult time will give her strength to meet the challenges of life after graduation, whether it be marriage, work or college. She will have the ability to forge ahead rather than look to the past.

9
ADULTHOOD

When my daughters were young, I was fortunate enough to have several friends who had teenage daughters. Without exception, the loveliest girls were the ones who were brought up in an atmosphere of warmth, friendliness and freedom. The mothers themselves may have had their own problems with their parents, but they enjoyed their daughters and their daughters were enjoyable. Each child in those homes was treated as an individual and was appreciated for who she was. They were given solid guidance from their parents as youngsters, and as teenagers were given the opportunity to test the values they had learned. They were made to feel an integral and important part of their homes. They were allowed to have input into what affected them and their family. They were treated with respect, and as a result they treated their parents and others with respect.

You should always be honest with your daughter about your feelings. Don't put her in the position of having to lie to you. Forbid as little as possible. Let your daughter know you trust her, and act as if you do. Give your daughter reason to trust you. If she does, she will be more likely to trust your judgment. Keep your word to her, and when you cannot, tell her and explain why not. Don't make excuses for your petty reasons, either. You are entitled to them, and there's no reason for your daughter to think you're perfect any more than for you to expect her to be perfect.

At times your daughter will seem very, very strange to you. Learn to tolerate some strangeness. Have enough personal self-confidence to recognize the difference between problem behavior requiring professional help and everyday adolescent peculiarities.

Let your daughter put as much space between the two of you as she needs to stand on her own and grow to maturity. If you don't, she will spend a good part of her adult life still trying to separate herself from you and to prove herself to you . . . and you will have denied yourself the pleasure of her adult friendship.

ABOUT THE AUTHORS

Meryl Fishman, a native New Yorker, is the mother of two teen-age daughters. She is a graduate of Pace University and is currently earning a law degree at New York Law School.

Kathleen Horwich, also a native New Yorker, is the mother of one teenage daughter. She is a graduate of Columbia University and the author of *My First Picture Dictionary* and *My First Picture Word Book*.

INDEX

Rebelliousness, 22–23
Rebuffs, 17–18
Reclusiveness, 40
Recognition
  and confidence-building, 29
  of fears, 33
Records, 25, 61
Redecorating, 132
Refereeing, with siblings, 100
Regional dress styles, 43
Rejection, and unwed motherhood,
  116
Rejection letters (college), 92–93
Relationships, 97–110
  daughter-father conflicts,
    100–101
  destructive, 108
  living with father, 102
  mother-daughter, 97–98
  only child, 98–99
  siblings, 99–100
  stepmother problems, 103–6
  see also Friends; Relatives
Relatives, 102, 106–7, 116
Religion, 143–44
Remarriage, see Second marriage
Respect, 159
  as communication, 47, 48
Responsibility (instilling), and
    parental role, 59–71
  babysitting, 65–66
  chores, 59–60
  curfews, 63–65
  driving, 66–67
  money, 61–62
  staying alone, 69–70
  voting, 70–71
  working, 67–68
Responsibility (sense of), 29–30
  and homework, 85
  see also Decision making
"Right" way, to bring up
    adolescents, 14
Rudeness, 17–18, 19
Rule bending, 135–36
Running away from home, 126–27

Safety
  and curfews, 63–64
  and staying alone, 69
  see also Dangers
Sanitary napkins, 72
Savings, 96
  for emergencies, 142
Saying no, as discipline, 14, 53–55
Scapegoat, mother as, 108
School, 84–89
  and absentmindedness, 23
  and babysitting, 66
  cheating at, 136–37
  dropping out, 87–89
  and fearfulness, 36
  grades, 85–87
  homework, 84–85
  and illness, 141
  insolence at, 18
  see also Boarding school; Senior
    high-school year
School functions, 149–50
Screaming, 52
Second marriage, 131–32
Secretiveness, 40
Security, at home, 90
Self-assertiveness, 29
Self-assurance, and dressing up, 31
Self-centered phase, 129
  see also Selfishness
Self-confidence, building, 29–31
Self-consciousness
  of boys, 76
  and exercise, 73–74
  about menstruation, 76–77
Self-discipline, 61
Self-esteem, 38–39
  and dieting, 82
Self-image, 22
Selfishness, 36–38
  right to, 54–55
Self-respect, 38–39, 47
Self-worth, 47, 61
  and drug addiction, 121
Senior high-school year, 157–58
Separation anxiety, 110

171